FUNCTIONAL LIVING GOD'S WAY

Achieving Abundant Living
Through Biblical Principles

W. E. HUNTER

Evangelist

Copyright © 2010 by W. E. Hunter

Functional Living God's Way
by W. E. Hunter

Printed in the United States of America

ISBN 9781615798308

All rights reserved solely by the author. The author guarantees all contents are original and do not infringe upon the legal rights of any other person or work. No part of this book may be reproduced in any form without the permission of the author. The views expressed in this book are not necessarily those of the publisher.

Unless otherwise indicated, Bible quotations are taken from the New American Standard Bible®. Copyright © 1960, 1962, 1963, 1968, 1971, 1972, 1973, 1975, 1977 by The Lockman Foundation. Used by permission.

Scripture quotations marked NKJV are taken from the New King James Version. Copyright © 1982 by Thomas Nelson, Inc. Used by permission. All rights reserved.

Scripture quotations marked NLT are taken from the New Living Translation, copyright © 1996, 2004. Used by permission of Tyndale House Publishers, Inc., Wheaton, Illinois 60189. All rights reserved.

www.xulonpress.com

To Bert Hunter, my wife, my lover, and my friend, whose faith, love, and heart have been a constant compass for me and whose commitment, support, and sustaining strength have been a blessing to me and my efforts to preach Jesus.

Contents

Preface ix

Chapter 1:
Unrealized Opportunities 11

Chapter 2:
The True Information from the True Source 14

Chapter 3:
The All-Sufficiency of the Bible
(Part 1) 22

Chapter 4:
The All-Sufficiency of the Bible
(Part 2) 30

Chapter 5:
The All-Sufficiency of the Bible
(Part 3) 35

Chapter 6:
Change: God's Principles Versus Man's Theories
(Part 1) 38

Chapter 7:
Change: God's Principles Versus Man's Theories
(Part 2) 47

Chapter 8:
Change: God's Principles Versus Man's Theories
(Part 3) 51

Chapter 9:
Change: God's Principles Versus Man's Theories
(Part 4) 65

Chapter 10:
Change: God's Principles Versus Man's Theories
(Part 5) 79

Chapter 11:
Change: God's Principles Versus Man's Theories
(Part 6) 92

Reflections..101

Questions for Study..103

Endnotes and Bibliography..123

Preface

Psychologist Gary Collins wrote, "Regretfully, many Christians do not feel very loving and neither do their words or actions express a loving attitude. Many feel defeated by sin, internal conflicts, and the pressures of life. Some are frustrated because their growth seems to be so slow. Others are concerned because their lives seem so joyless, there is no 'sparkle' in their worship, and they are caught in a net of 'spiritual dryness.' They read the Bible but words seem dull and irrelevant. They pray, more out of habit than desire, but their prayers seem unanswered. They want to do good and to love, but their actions aren't very loving and their consciences seem insensitive and blunted."[1]

The conditions Collins described exist in every congregation of the Lord's people. And despite all that Christians have going for them—all the spiritual blessings God gives in Christ Jesus, the infallible guidance of God's Word given to His people, the invincible power of God's Holy Spirit living in each Christian—the conditions exist in increasingly larger numbers.

Many, though in the company of scores of people each day, live lives of unwanted aloneness and loneliness because of their inability to establish and maintain fulfilling relationships. Others are unable to enjoy the things they have because of a belief that their lives would be more fulfilling if they only had this, that, or some other thing. Still others struggle through defeated lives caused by retrieving past defeats, disappointments, and wrongs both done and suffered, and by pulling from the future unwanted events that they fear might happen. Finally, for far too many, life is nothing more than one massive period of agonizing frustrations and doubts because of the incompatibility between the life they desire and the values by which they live.

Such conditions exist despite the fact that many of those who suffer from them have applied numerous highly acclaimed principles espoused in multitudes of books, articles, tapes, and other media venues. Notwithstanding the fact that these principles are from the minds of highly educated and experienced authors, they rarely produce a lasting quality of improvement, and they never produce true fulfillment. The reason is quite simple: human wisdom is incapable of correctly identifying and effectively addressing the problems within an individual and between individuals. Only God can. The following material is designed to address the problems leading to dysfunctional living and to provide God's formula for *functional living*.

Chapter 1

Unrealized Opportunities

On the journey from slavery in Egypt to the promised land of Canaan, Moses informed the Israelites that God had waiting for them "great and splendid cities which you did not build, and houses full of good things which you did not fill, and hewn cisterns which you did not dig, vineyards and olives trees which you did not plant" (Deut. 6:10–11). Nevertheless, the Israelites would wander in the wilderness for more than forty years before experiencing the bountiful blessings stored for them in Canaan. Why? The answer is simple: because of their failure to trust God and to act according to His word to them (Numbers 13–14; Heb. 3:16–19).

The Israelites had the opportunity for comfortable living in well-stocked cities in Canaan, but instead they chose a harsh life of wilderness wandering. One of the saddest testimonies of our day is the fact that despite the many blessings God has provided in Jesus Christ, all too many Christians are living significantly below their blessing. Like the Israelites of old, many Christians are failing to seize the opportunities God has already provided.

Grand Deception

In his exhortations in 2 Corinthians, the apostle Paul references Satan and his schemes; that is, the machinations of Satan's mind (2:11). Another prominent name the New Testament gives to this fallen angel is "the devil" (Matt. 4:1). Regardless of the name used, the Scriptures are very explicit in pointing out the role and the aim of this fallen angel.

As an adversary, Satan opposes God and everything good. As the false accuser, his tactics involve casting himself or something else between God and His children for the purpose of separating them. One of his grandest deceptions in recent centuries is that of convincing many people that the Bible has no place in addressing their personal problems. He has convinced many that the Bible has its place in explaining the interactions of God with the ancient Israelites and the nations with whom Israel came in contact, for explaining the existence of the institution known as the church and the distinctive nature of the Christian faith, and for use as a guide for those who engage in the act of Christian worship. But in the area of human problems, he has convinced them that the Bible is ill equipped to address living effective and fulfilled lives in a scientific and modern world. Regretfully, in recent decades, all too many Christians and Christian churches have fallen prey to this damnable scheme.

The 10/90 Rule

Two cardinal facts of the Christian faith are as follows: (1) Christ Jesus came to earth to make it possible for all who believe in Him and His message to live with God eternally (John 3:14–17), and (2) Jesus came to give life in its fullest measure here on earth (John 10:9–10). Unfortunately, although most Christians sincerely accept both these facts, they struggle somewhat to realize the second. While feeling secure in their eternal life in heaven, they struggle to experience the fullness of life here on earth. Although God neither desires nor makes provision for such a state, it is nonetheless a common experience for all too many of God's children.

Why is that true? Many would point to the conditions in the world in which we live as the culprit. Death, disease, disappointments, defeats—and on the list goes—rob people of the enjoyment of a full life. Such conditions, however, are facts of life shared by all. Who among us has not experienced the truth of Job's lament: "Man that is born of woman is short-lived and full of turmoil" (Job 14:1; see also Eccles. 2:22–23; 5:17)? Jesus made provisions for living the full life, knowing exactly what the conditions in each age would be. Furthermore, in spite of adverse conditions in the world, there have been people in each age of human history who have enjoyed life to its fullest. No, conditions are not the real cause.

The real cause lies in how one chooses to respond to those conditions, how one programs oneself to respond to life's situations. As Charles Swindoll says, the "10/90 rule" is at work every day in every situation. Simply stated, this principle says that life is 10 percent what happens to us and 90 percent what we make of what happens to us. [2] Unfortunately, many Christians choose to respond to life's circumstances in ways that often exacerbate the situation and, more often than not, diminish the true quality of their lives.

Chapter 2

The True Information from the True Source

Generally, the choices a person makes—be they good choices or bad choices—are functions of the information he possesses and the way that information is processed. One's choices become dysfunctional choices primarily because of a lack of effective information or ineffective processing of that information. In turn, these dysfunctional choices lead to dysfunctional living. Effective information, therefore, is required to make the type of choices that bring life back to its God-intended state.

By effective information, I mean true information that is resident not just in the mind but also in a person's spirit and soul and that contains within itself the power to change. This raises two vital and interrelated questions: (1) what is the source of such information, and (2) by what authority is the information commended? In his *Biblical Solutions to Contemporary Problems,* Rus Walton refers to George Marston's statement in Marston's *Voice of Authority* that "every man has a standard in matters of truth and conduct. That is his voice of authority."[3]

Every person relies on one of two sources as his voice of authority. Either he looks to the omnipotent, omnivisual, omniscient, omnipresent God who created humans, knows all about them, and knows what it takes to live life in its fullness in this sin-cursed world; or he looks to the mind of fallen, sin-cursed, fallible humans (Genesis 1; Ps. 139:1–13; 14:1–3; 58:3; Eph. 2:1–3; 4:17–19). Since there are but two sources of information from which to draw, the vital question each Christian must ask is, who is my voice of authority and my source of information: the infallible God or fallible man?

The adverse conditions humans face today are the result of human wisdom throughout history—wisdom that is a combination of input from the ideas of great thinkers, the writings of literary giants, the findings of esteemed scientists, and the pronouncements of revered church leaders. However, no matter the combination of sources, it remains unaided human wisdom from below; it is not from God, but is earthly, natural, demonic, and untrustworthy (James 3:13–18; 1 Cor. 2:5; 3:19).

Only the wisdom that comes from God through the Holy Spirit–inspired and Holy Spirit–empowered written Word can lay claim to the wisdom from above. The Bible teaches that man was made for God (Rev. 4:11) and is dependent on Him (Acts 17:28). These two facts alone make the God-given Word (the Bible) indispensable to man's ability to find real fulfillment (Matt. 4:4).

Authenticity

Since many humans were used in the writing of the books of the Bible, and since many humans were involved in copying those same books over many centuries, and since humans are capable of making mistakes and *do* make mistakes, how can one be sure that the Bible we have today agrees with what was originally written? This is an extremely important question because it addresses the validity of one authority over another. If the Bible we have today is not consistent with what was originally breathed from God, then its contents are no different than the contents of any other message, and it has no legitimate basis to either exert its message over any other message or to make the types of demands for change it makes. In other words, the question is, how authentic is the Christian Bible?

The issue of authenticity is one with which doubters often confront Christians and one by which the faith of more than a few Christians has been shaken. It deals with the issue of whether the Bible we have today accurately reflects what was originally written. While it is true that not a single document in existence today was written or dictated by the authors to whom the writing of the Bible is attributed, Christians can be confident that the Bible we use today is, in fact, extremely close to those originally inspired written or dictated manuscripts. Let's take a closer look at some of the facts that support such a statement.

1. Old Testament manuscripts: Although only a few Old Testament manuscripts are in existence (the earliest of which dates from the tenth century AD), and despite the fact that only one of these is complete, the accuracy of the copies of the Old Testament is supported by other evidence. First, all of the manuscripts, no matter who prepared them or where they were found, agree to a great extent. Such agreement between texts from Palestine, Syria, and Egypt suggests a strong and ancient original tradition.

Second, the manuscripts agree with another ancient source of the Old Testament, the Septuagint, which is the Greek translation of the Old Testament that dates from the second and third centuries BC. Finally, the Dead Sea Scrolls, written about a thousand years before the Old Testament manuscripts, provide an excellent basis of comparison that shows an astonishing reliability in transmission of text. All the evidence available reveals no substantial changes in the text of the Old Testament in the last two thousand years and very little change before that. [4]

2. New Testament manuscripts: The evidence for the New Testament is overwhelming. We have close to, if not more than, twenty-five thousand manuscripts and copies of portions of the New Testament in existence today, some of which date from the second and third centuries AD. No other document of antiquity comes close to that number. By way of comparison, for the most famous book of ancient Greece, those ancient Greek poems attributed to Homer and known as *The Iliad,* there are only 643 copies. Of Julius Caesar's *Gallic Wars,* commentaries depicting the Romans' conquest of Gaul (modern-day France, parts of Belgium, western Germany, and northern Italy), there are but ten copies, the earliest of which was produced a thousand years after the original. Nevertheless, no serious doubts have been raised concerning the authenticity of either of these famous documents. Having such a large number of copies of the New Testament, some dating to within seventy years of the original documents, is, therefore, undoubtedly amazing.

True, many small differences exist among all the existing manuscripts of the New Testament. However, of the ten thousand places where variations (not errors, as skeptics and critics claim) occur, most are matters of spelling and the order of words. There are less than forty places in the New Testament where scholars are really not certain which reading is original; however, not one of these has any effect on any central doctrine of the faith. We can be assured, therefore, that we have 100 percent of the New Testament and are certain of 99.5 percent of it. The fact is, even if all the copies of the New Testament had been burned at the end of the third century, scholars assure us that we could know virtually all of the New Testament (except for approximately eleven verses, mostly from 2 and 3 John) by studying the quotations in the writings of the church fathers of the second and third centuries.[5]

3. Conclusion: We can be assured that the Bible we have today is God speaking to us. Such assurance rests on the fact that we have a great deal of evidence to show that the current-day Bible, like no other book from the ancient world, represents the original manuscripts with a very high degree of accuracy. Thus Christians who accept the principles for functional, abundant living contained in the Bible do not have to fall prey to the doubters and skeptics who reject the teachings of the Bible or seek to add human wisdom to it. They can effectively debunk the claim that the inspiration applied only to the original writings, which we do not have, and correct the erroneous conclusion that the reliability of its teachings leaves much room for needed insertions and deletions.

Bible Translations

The Bible we have today reflects almost total accuracy to the original manuscripts written or dictated by those whom God inspired to deliver His words, but with the multiplicity of translations available, care must be taken in selecting a translation to use. Not all translations of the Bible retain an extremely close accuracy to the original inspired manuscripts. Following is a listing of the major categories of translations available today as explained on pages 12–13 in *Why Is My Choice of a Bible Translation So Important?* by Wayne Grudem and Jerry Thacker.

1. Essentially literal (word for word): An essentially literal translation "strives to translate the exact words of the original-language text in a translation, but not in such a rigid way as to violate the normal rules of language and syntax" of the language from which the translation comes and the language into which it is being translated. The English Standard Version, New American Standard Bible, King James Version, New King James Version, Revised Standard Version, New Revised Standard Version, and New English Translation fit into this category.

2. Dynamic equivalence (thought for thought): A dynamic-equivalence translation seeks to reproduce the thoughts or ideas of the original text in the way a modern speaker would say them; that is, it seeks to translate the original-language text into the targeted language in terms of a meaning that corresponds, or is equivalent, to a meaning in the original-language text. In this category are the New Living Translation, the New Century Version, the Revised English Version, and the Good News Bible.

3. Paraphrase: A paraphrase translation takes even more liberties than a dynamic-equivalence translation in how it renders biblical passages, frequently finding creative new ways to express the general idea of the verse. The Message, The Living Bible, the New Testament in Modern English, and the Good News Bible fit into this category.

4. Mixed versions: This category of translation does not fall precisely into any of the above three categories. It is a mixture of two types: it contains substantial elements of a dynamic-equivalence translation mixed with a basic commitment to an essentially literal translation. In this category are the New International Version and Today's New International Version.

5. Gender neutral: Depending on their advocates, translations in this category are also called "gender accurate" and "gender inclusive." In this category, translators have changed thousands of verses by removing the male-oriented words *father, son, brother, man,* and *he/him/his.* The problem represented here is that the changes occur in places where the use of these words was good; that is, in accurate translations of the original Greek or Hebrew. This results in the translation of the general idea of the passages, but with the omission of male-oriented details of meaning. The New Revised Standard Version, Today's New International Version, New Century Version, Good News Bible Today, and the Contemporary English Version fit into this category of translation.

Dangerous Focus

In the last several decades, a major focus of many Bible translators has been the desire to translate the Bible into more contemporary expressions that make it more attractive to the masses. Such efforts do, in fact, produce translations easier to read and more attractive to the masses; however, contained therein are two joint dangers: (1) the translations are colored by the translator's own opinions, and (2) preference is given to what is more palatable to the modern reader than to words and phrases that more accurately reflect the intent of the original authors. Those are exactly the two dangers by which a number of modern-day translations have been afflicted. Therefore, it is of the utmost importance that any translation must be held to the standard of accurately representing in English what the original Hebrew and Greek languages conveyed to the original audience.

Choosing which Bible to read and to trust is an important decision. Christians need to care enough about their own sanctification to choose a translation that conveys the very words of God. They should look for a Bible that they can use and trust as a daily study Bible. No matter how antiquated the expressions might be, every word God has spoken to us is important (2 Tim. 3:16; 2 Pet. 1:20–21; Prov. 30:5; Matt. 4:4).

The Bible teaches that God's thoughts and ways are significantly different from and significantly above the thoughts and ways of humans (Isa. 55:8–9); therefore, no human or group of humans (that is, translators) can claim to completely understand the depth of meaning of the words God has breathed out. Remember, a translation containing words or concepts that the masses find easy to understand but are not accurate reflections of the very words of God will have harmful effects on one's ability to live the life Jesus gives and to cope with the many crises life presents.

Conclusion

No Christian should take lightly the decision of which Bible translation to choose. In simple terms, to achieve the results God has promised (Ps. 19:7–11; 119:98–100; 2 Tim. 3:16–17), the counsel one obeys must be contained in a translation that conveys the very words of God.

Chapter 3

The All-Sufficiency of the Bible (Part 1)

As one travels the road to truly functional living, a critical juncture arises regarding the acceptance of the fact that in His Holy Spirit–inspired Word, God has provided all the principles needed to experience life in its fullest measure. God's instructions are complete, needing no modification of any type. It is at this juncture that many Christians today encounter another of Satan's deceptions.

Prevalent Beliefs

Even after resolving the issue of the authenticity of the Bible we have today and navigating through the many modern-day translations to arrive at one that accurately conveys the very words of God, there are yet more hurdles confronting Christians who desire to honor God. The following beliefs are widespread in both the larger community of our culture and in the Christian community:

1. Inappropriate use: Some insist that the plan and purpose of the Bible was not designed for addressing the problems for which people need professionally trained counselors. Therefore, they say, one cannot—nay, must not—seek to use the Bible for such purpose.

2. Combining: In their objections to the idea that the Bible is fully equipped to address the problems of humans in this highly complex age in which we live, some critics point to the advances in human knowledge and of their interactions. Such knowledge, they reason, was not known when the Bible was written. They posit that the present-day knowledge of man and his world is better able to effectively speak to his issues; thus, the best results are achieved by combining both the principles contained in the Bible and the practical insights from modern-day sciences. Therefore, they conclude, combining provides a solid approach to dealing with the many problems of living in today's world.

3. There all the time: To address those unable to accept the idea of adding anything to the principles contained in the Bible, some critics espouse the view that the principles put forth by the various sciences consist of instructions that have been included in God's Word all along; the church is just belatedly discovering them, they say. Given the incursion that postmodern thinking has made among members of the church, such thinking is finding an increasing number of adherents.

4. Ineffective results: Another objection to the all-sufficiency of the Bible to address human problems is often stated thusly: "If the Bible is all-sufficient in addressing the dysfunctions within a person and between people, why are so many Christians living dysfunctional lives?"

Reshaping the Faith

One explanation to the success achieved by the above objections lies in the incursion into the church of various humanistic doctrines and the syncretistic shaping of many Christians' belief systems. (An example of this syncretistic shaping is seen in the 2009 "defrocking" of a Seattle, Washington, Episcopal priest who announced that she is both Christian and Muslim).[6]

Listed below are some of these specific doctrines and schools of thought:

1. Humanism: Humanism is a doctrine, attitude, or way of life centered on human interests or values; it is a philosophy that usually rejects supernaturalism and stresses an individual's dignity and worth and his capacity for self-realization through reason. Secular humanists believe moral values derive from human experience and that ethics are autonomous and situational, needing no theological or ideological sanction. Furthermore, it is the belief that in order to enhance personal freedom and dignity, the individual must experience a full range of civil liberties in all societies.

Unfortunately, some—and perhaps many—of the theories spawned from this philosophy and prevalent in society today are generally accepted by many Christians as basic common sense and harmless fact. The truth is, however, when those theories are closely examined against the principles contained in God's written Word, it becomes clear that much of what is presented as a solution to individual and collective dysfunctions is contrary to and hostile toward the Word of God.

2. Political correctness: Perhaps more readily accepted than all the other ideas is that of political correctness. *Merriam-Webster's Dictionary* defines *political correctness* as "conforming to a belief that language and practices which could offend political sensibilities (as in matters of sex or race) should be eliminated." [7] While the concept appears to be aimed at eliminating words and actions designed to offend and to unlawfully exclude people, its real effect is the creation of an environment of ever-increasing pressure for everyone to conform to the prevailing opinions, values, and standards of the dominant culture.

Consequently, it is politically correct to describe an unmarried man and woman who are living together as merely people of the opposite sex who are sharing living quarters. Political correctness dictates the use of "gay" rather than "homosexual" and "pro-choice" rather than "pro-abortion." It describes a person as "physically challenged," rather than saying the person has a "physical handicap."

"What's the big deal?" some would ask. "They are only words." But words influence the way people think; and since thoughts determine action, there is a direct and powerful connection between the words people use and the actions they subsequently take. As a result, political correctness has evolved to the wide acceptance of the active belief that every idea is to be tolerated because no idea (including ideas of religion) is better than any other idea, thus leading to the conclusion that everything, including truth, is relative. This, in turn, has led to ever-increasing pressure (legal and otherwise) to abandon the teachings of the Bible that others might find offensive or otherwise exclusive, and many Christians, unfortunately, have yielded to this pressure. Acceptance of political correctness has also led many Christians to modify their beliefs concerning good and bad, right and wrong, acceptable and unacceptable behavior—issues to which God in His Word has clearly spoken.

One example of the pervasiveness of political correctness today involves a Pentecostal pastor in Kalmar, Sweden, who was sentenced to one month in prison on the charge of inciting hatred against homosexuals. The pastor was convicted for comments rendered in a sermon drawn from biblical texts dealing with the subject.[8] Another example involves a Lutheran church located near a major city thoroughfare, whose membership voted to remove the symbol of the cross from its building because it might offend non-Christians or those whose religion did not honor the cross.[9]

As taught in His Word, God has made the church "the pillar and foundation of the truth" (1 Tim. 3:15), and His Word is truth (John 17:17); consequently, any "truth" that contradicts God's Word is, by such contradiction, not truth. Therefore, Christians must hold to and hold up the Word of God at all cost, regardless of society's expectations, desires, and dictates.

As Christians, we are God's representatives in the world and thus mandated to deport ourselves according to the wisdom of God's Word. In so doing, we convict the world of its wayward actions (Eph. 5:1–17) and lead it to acknowledge God and give Him the honor due (Matt. 5:13–16). As God's representatives in and to the world, we are instructed to not let the world shape us by its behavior, but rather to be transformed by the renewal that comes from God's Word through the ministry of the Holy Spirit (Rom. 12:1–2; Titus 3:1–5).

3. Subjectivism: The concept of political correctness is but one of the widely believed principles that many Christians have readily accepted. The concept of subjectivism has also received wide acceptance and is gaining adherents within the community of God. Subjectivism is the belief that there are few, if any, objective principles of conduct and that those that do exist do not apply to all people in all situations. In other words, subjectivism is the denial of absolute standards of morality.

The concept of subjectivism is founded in the belief that ethical values are individual choices and thus subjective in nature. It makes the individual who originates the behavior the one who also determines the rightness or wrongness of the behavior. The benchmark of the moral value of any behavior is based entirely on the individual's perceptions, opinions, experiences, inclinations, and desires of right and wrong. In short, whatever an individual thinks is right is right, and whatever he thinks is wrong is wrong.

In subjectivism, because the individual is the referee, and because there are billions of individuals, there can be no such thing as an absolute, unchanging, universal standard of conduct. Consequently, through the elimination of absolutes, subjectivism reduces morality to individual taste and feeling. Again, by making the individual the basis of morality, subjectivism makes it possible for all to be right and for none to be wrong. In other words, in the eyes of those who hold to it, this theory makes it possible for a person to be always correct in his ethical views.

4. Relativism: Closely aligned with the above two concepts, both in its effects on society at large and its impact on the church, is the concept of relativism. This philosophy espouses two main tenets: (1) all truth is relative to the individual, and (2) each worldview contains it own logic and truth and is, therefore, equally true. Existing under the umbrella of relativism are such categories as the following:

a. *Ethical relativism* teaches that morality is relative to the norms of a specific culture. Whether an action is considered right or wrong depends on the moral norms of the culture in which the action is practiced. Consequently, there are no standards of morality or ethics that can be universally applied to all people at all times. In other words, the only moral or ethical standards against which a society's actions can be judged are its own.

b. *Situational relativism* teaches that there are no absolutes regarding right and wrong and other values of a moral nature; all is relative. The designations of "good" and "bad" are designations attached to beliefs and actions by the culture in which one lives. When something is considered good, it simply means that it is socially approved in that culture by the majority over a period of time. The same is true of something considered bad. Consequently, no belief or action is inherently good or bad; it is merely accepted or not accepted within that given culture.

c. *Cognitive relativism* teaches that all truth is relative and that no system of truth is more valid than any other system of truth. There exists, therefore, no objective standard of truth. Furthermore, it states that truth is determined by ways of reasoning unique to an individual culture, thus eliminating the possibility of a universal standard of truth and a universal giver of truth. It teaches that religious truths are not actually found in Scripture; rather, they are formulated in the human mind from Scripture. Consequently, this theory implies that the authority of Scripture is not derived from the conviction that God spoke it, but from the fact that the church constructed a belief from what God spoke.

5. Pluralism: The concept of pluralism is perhaps second only to the concept of political correctness in its general acceptance by professing Christians. Why is this? This is probably because many people believe that pluralism simply deals with diversity and tolerance, both of which are necessary to successful living in society. However, pluralism is more—much more.

Pluralism contains, as do other humanistic theories, the belief that absolute truth does not exist. It also teaches that truth is relative and that the ideas of right and wrong depend on the subjective assessments of humans. It is the notion that all religious beliefs, systems, and philosophies are of equal validity; therefore, all religions must be constructed so that none of their doctrines or values offend followers of other religions.

The concept of pluralism also includes the belief that each of the world's religions offers a different yet valid way to salvation. According to pluralism, other religions are not secondary or inferior to the Christian religion, but rather, they are independent, authentic paths to "the divine."

Chapter 4

The All-Sufficiency of the Bible (Part 2)

The Bible Unmixed

What have been the results of all these various beliefs with which Christians are constantly bombarded? In the belief systems of many, a sort of syncretism has taken place. In this context, syncretism refers to changes in a Christian's beliefs and practices through conscious and unconscious attempts to accommodate to the culture in which he lives. These attempts to accommodate flow from two main sources: (1) the desire of the Christian to present his message and beliefs in a way more acceptable and attractive to the larger culture, and (2) the failure of many Christians to maintain a worldview formulated by God's eternal truths, thus leading to the acceptance of many of the major assumptions of the larger society.

Christians must believe that God's Word is the ultimate standard of truth. In John 17:17, Jesus prayed to His Father, "Sanctify them in the truth; Your word is truth." Jesus did not use the adjective *true;* rather, He used a noun to emphasize that God's Word is not simply true, but is truth itself. In other words, the Bible is not true in the sense that it conforms to some higher standard of truth, but rather, the Bible is itself the final standard of truth.

The Bible is God's word to us and is the ultimate standard of what is true and what is not true. God's Word is truth itself; consequently, the Bible is the reference point by which every other claim to truthfulness must be measured. Christians must be watchful for and reject any instructions that mix or confuse human words with God's words.

In very clear terms, God issued warnings against mixing human words with His words (Jer. 23:28; Deut. 4:2; 12:32; Prov. 30:6). In the New Testament, Jesus condemned the Pharisees and teachers of the law who put their own teachings ahead of God's words (Matt. 15:3). Therefore, while seeking to influence the world for Christ, Christians must faithfully adhere to the Holy Spirit's warning to carefully heed the things delivered "once for all . . . to the saints" (Jude 3; see also Heb. 2:1). By so doing, Christians will effectively fulfill God's design for them to change the popular culture in which they live without being changed by that culture (Rom. 12:1–2).

The Peril of Christian Counseling

Even when Christians work diligently to avoid embracing humanistic theories that pollute the principles by which they seek to live functional, abundant lives, many, nevertheless, fall prey to numerous humanistic theories in different disguises. Much of this falls under the umbrella of what is termed "Christian counseling." Listed below are two main aspects that need to be considered further:

1. Much of Christian counseling is based largely on human wisdom. One can understand this peril better by realizing that the modern-day counseling industry, including much of so-called Christian counseling, is based largely on the work of Sigmund Freud, the father of psychoanalysis. In developing his theories, Freud drew heavily on the theory of evolution developed by Charles Darwin (yes, *that* Charles Darwin). The theories of these two men, theories that have so shaped our society, are products of man's fallen nature and thus totally at enmity with God. The men who developed these foundational theories were motivated by an unflinching desire to not honor or recognize the Creator God and His revealed word to man. Their aim was to render the belief in the Creator as unnecessary to both functional living and explaining the existence of the universe.

At their cores, the theories of evolution and psychoanalysis are much more than the mere rejection of the existence of the Creator God, His words, and His supernatural influence on and in the universe. They are also socially and scientifically acceptable expressions to humanity's age-old striving to be like God. This striving began in Eden with Adam and Eve's dissatisfaction with God's wisdom and their acceptance of Satan's lie that by ignoring God's law and doing what seemed good to them, they could be like God (Gen. 3:1–6).

The theory of evolution posits that the success of human development through its various stages was a function of properly aligned environmental conditions and that without that alignment, humans would not have become the successful beings they are today. In developing the theory of psychoanalysis, Freud replicated this concept with the idea that the proper type, quantity, and quality of environmental stimuli are required for humans to develop properly and live successfully in the community of other beings.

2. Much of Christian counseling is not Christian. As one carefully examines the presuppositions upon which psychotherapy in all of its various forms is based, complete agreement with the present-day postmodern mind-set of the dominant society is clearly seen. These two, modern-day psychoanalysis and postmodernity (along with Darwin's theory of evolution), have greatly influenced the thinking of many Christians. The areas of agreement as categorized by Gary L. Almy in his book *How Christian Is Christian Counseling?* are as follows: [10]

a. *Denial of God and His Word:* In place of the recognition of God—through whose power and by whose Word all are sustained and to whom all are accountable—both schools of thought deny God's existence altogether or make man his own god. By so doing, they place reliance for control and guidance on the individual, rather than on a power beyond the individual, such as the Creator God.

b. *Denial of the applicability of God's Word:* Denying the claim that God's Word represents His timeless and firm truth to be accepted in its entirety, both views assert that no text is timeless and firm in its meaning; therefore, people are free to pick and choose the parts that resonate with their own sense of truth and falsity, right and wrong.

c. *Knowledge sourced in individual experience:* Both teach that knowledge exists not independently of subjective experience, but only through, and limited by, subjective experience.

d. *Humans as captive to their environment:* In these two worldviews, humans are not free to make undetermined choices; rather, their responses are predetermined by prior environmental conditions. In other words, humans are victims of forces beyond their control—forces exerted upon them during critical times in their mental, emotional, psychological, and spiritual development.

e. *The needs of the individual as paramount:* Instead of seeing humans as interrelated and interdependent creatures responsible to and for one another, both teach that all values, rights, and duties originate with the individual; therefore, the interests and needs of the individual are paramount.

f. *No universal standard of morality:* In both, there is no established standard of morality applicable to all people in all situations; rather, morality is determined by one's personal preferences. The individual preferences become both the standard and the validation for morality.

g. *Humans as products of their environment:* Finally, common to both worldviews is the belief that humans are passive products of their environments. In other words, because man is the product of his environment, he is not responsible for his own individual actions; rather, his inherited traits and the environment in which he developed are totally responsible for what he is and what he does.

Chapter 5

The All-Sufficiency of the Bible (Part 3)

The Perfect Work of the Holy Spirit

Central to success in achieving functional living is acceptance of the Bible as God's instruction, inspired through the Holy Spirit, to His creatures as to how such living is achieved. Central to such acceptance is the belief that the work of the Holy Spirit is perfect within itself. Acceptance of these two tenets leads to the following conclusions:

1. The work of the Holy Spirit is incompatible with human works: Christians who depend on biblical principles as the source of knowledge for a functional life rely on principles that are products of the ministry of the Holy Spirit and contained in words inspired by the holy, omniscient, onmivisual, omnipresent, and omnipotent God. Nonbiblical principles (including much of what is called Christian counseling) rest on products of unholy, fallen human wisdom that not only seek to disavow God but also, by their very natures, are hostile to God. The former is from above and is heavenly, but the latter is earthly, at the mercy of and from the human mind. It follows the wishes of the lower nature (Eph. 2:1–3) — a nature that cannot understand the things of God (2 Cor. 2:14), contains no good thing (Rom. 7:18), and cannot please God (Rom. 8:6–8). Human wisdom always creates divisions, inhibits spiritual maturity, and hinders the ability of humans to know God (2 Cor. 2:14). These factors alone clearly highlight the inherent incompatibility of any principles different from those contained in the Bible with the work of the Holy Spirit.

2. The work of the Holy Spirit cannot be improved: There are any numbers of things that can be added to, subtracted from, or otherwise changed in order to bring about improvements. However, that which is perfect neither needs change nor can it be changed and still remain in its condition of perfection. By the very act of implementing a change, regardless of the nature of the change, that which was perfect becomes imperfect; that is, it loses its uniqueness.

The Holy Spirit declares God's Word as perfect in its origin, being, operation, and duration (Ps. 19:7; 119:160; James 1:25). Additionally, the Holy Spirit gives assurance that God's Word is able to make one wise, proficient, and thoroughly equipped for effective living in this world (Ps. 119:97–104; 2 Tim. 3:15–17); and He pronounces dire consequences upon those who attempt to add to or take from God's Word (Deut. 4:2; 12:32; Prov. 30:6; Rev. 22:18). Furthermore, regardless of the complete exegesis and application of Isaiah 55:8–9, one fact is abundantly plain: no matter how seemingly erudite, soothing, promise-filled, and comforting, the theories of humans are not God's theories and are immeasurably inferior.

3. The work of the Holy Spirit is sufficient unto itself: Notwithstanding the unquestioned superiority of biblical principles, far too many so-called Christian counselors and

Christian psychologists accept the false belief that nonbiblical counseling theories are both valuable and indispensable to the resolution of the many destructive problems humans encounter daily. Therefore, their approach to counseling is, in reality, nonbiblical, with a few biblical principles added for good measure. The result of such blending is the blurring—and in some cases the removing—of the irreconcilable distinction between the product of divine wisdom and the products of human wisdom.

In such cases, human wisdom eventually surpasses divine wisdom in importance and eventually wins out. Instead of conforming unbiblical principles to the Word of God, biblical principles are redefined in order to conform them to nonbiblical principles. The effects are analogous to what happens in the medical field when a quack comes up with an attractive treatment for a fatal disease. In too many cases, sick individuals place themselves under the care of the quack or commit to following an unproven regime involving the quack medicine; in so doing, they are led away from skilled physicians or legitimate medicine that can cure or lessen the effects of the ailment.

As stated earlier, the Holy Spirit declares God's Word to be all-sufficient for any eventuality. Because of its all-sufficient nature, truly functional living is dependent on nothing else. Christians must either consider that fact as true or reject it as untrue. When Christians make God's Word just another element among numerous nonbiblical elements, they not only consider the Bible deficient, but they also make the Bible self-contradictory, and thus untrustworthy and extraneous. In such cases, God's Word ceases to be ultimate truth and the absolute standard of what constitutes functional living.

Chapter 6

Change: God's Principles Versus Man's Theories (Part 1)

Perhaps the final choice one must make as he journeys toward truly functional living is whether to seek to bring about the needed changes through adherence to the principles inspired by the Holy Spirit and His ministry or to seek the needed changes through adherence to principles designed by human wisdom.

The Approach Is Critical

To achieve functional, abundant living requires change. How we Christians approach the task of achieving change, how we view human behavior, and how we determine the change needed are functions of what we believe about human nature. Our knowledge is derived either from our study of ourselves (the scientific study of the origin, the behavior, and the social and cultural development of human beings) or from God's view of us (our origin, nature, and future).

Absent an understanding and acceptance of what the Bible says about our origin, nature, and future, human wisdom develops a variety of explanations. However, it must be understood that man's views of his origin, nature, and future are contrary and incompatible with biblical teachings. Consequently, humans' nonbiblical views produce nonbiblical principles that, in turn, produce nonbiblical techniques in an effort to being about needed but misidentified change.

1. Good or bad? As a consequence of the failure to understand and accept the Bible's view of humankind's origin, nature, and future, all too many Christians have accepted the teaching that humans are basically good and come into this world as innocents with a natural disposition toward that which is good and pure. The Bible presents an entirely different picture, however. According to the Bible, humankind's problems are caused by sin, the sin that originated with Adam and Eve. As a result, all of Adam and Eve's progeny are born with a nature set against God and with the disposition to keep sinning (Gen. 8:21; Ps. 51:5; 58:3). Man's natural bent is to disbelieve God, to be his own god, and to admit and submit to no authority higher than himself.

2. External or internal? Human presuppositions and principles regarding change hold that man's behavior is the result of things that happen to him, things external to him. The person is not able to prevent their happening, and he is not able (aside from expert counselors) to effectively address their consequences. On the other hand, instead of condoning blame shifting, the Bible teaches that God hates man's attempt to deny his responsibility by shifting it to others (Ezek. 18:2–4, 20). God holds man responsible for what he does or what he fails to do (Rom. 14:10; 2 Cor. 5:10; James 2:10).

3. Sufficient or insufficient? In human nonbiblical theories of change, man is considered sufficient within himself;

that is, he has the resources within himself or within a group of his peers to solve his problems, thus permitting him to live up to his full potential. The Bible, on the other hand, reveals that it is God who works His will in man and that man is completely dependent on God for the resources he needs; they are not found in himself or in others.

4. Only from the Bible: Only from the Bible can one understand that true functional living comes only through knowing God, yielding to the ministry of the Holy Spirit, conforming to God's Holy Word, and fellowshiping with other believers in the church. Only from the Bible can one understand that man was created in the image of God (not evolved from a lower being), is dependent on God, and is answerable to God for how he lives his life (Eccles. 12:13–14).

The Bible is where God reveals His divine insights so that through the power of His Holy Spirit, we may live up to our God-intended potential. The Bible is where we find the true solutions to our real problems and the instructions that, if followed, will keep us out of trouble. The Bible is where we learn about proper relationships with God and with other humans. In it, God tells us what things are most important in life and how we can attain them, and how to seek and live happy and abundant lives.

As Vern S. Poythress and Wayne A. Grudem wrote in their *The TNIV and the Gender-Neutral Bible Controversy,* "We are to meditate on it continually. 'But his delight is in the law of the Lord, and on his law he *meditates* day and night' (Ps. 1:2, NIV). Meditation is appropriate to Scripture, because every detail, every word, every nuance of meaning comes to us from God himself, and nothing is to be missed. . . . These details of meaning also belong to Scripture, and along with all other details contribute to making it 'profitable' for us (2 Tim. 3:16)."[11]

5. Conclusion: When the Bible gives its solution to a problem or provides counsel as to how to prevent certain problems, no matter how difficult or how contrary to human wisdom such counsel may be, those who desire to honor God and to live true, functional, abundant lives can rest assured that the instructions given will produce the exact results God intended.

Functional Living

As stated previously, one charge leveled against the all-sufficiency of the Bible to address human ills is that if the Bible is really sufficient, why are there so many Christians living dysfunctional, unfulfilled lives? Sadly, many Christians do find Christian living drudgery.

Christians are sent to the world to show the type of love demonstrated by their Lord, who freely gave of Himself for those who not only did not deserve such love but who also were ungodly enemies (Rom. 5:6–10; Gal. 1:4; Titus 2:14). Furthermore, Christians are equipped to show such love by the Holy Spirit, who infuses this love of God into their hearts (Rom. 5:5). However, at the same time, many Christians do not feel very loving, and often their words or actions do not express a loving attitude. Many live joyless lives that are defeated by sin, internal conflict, and the pressures of life. No matter their commitment to God, no matter how diligently they try to live as God wills, no matter their resolve to live joyful lives, they do not experience the functional, abundant living they desire. Why?

1. Values and choice: A key to discovering the answers to and the resolutions for these regretful conditions so that a functional, abundant life becomes a reality lies in the understanding that a person's actions do not develop out of thin air, nor are they the results of a series of unconscious or accidental decisions. One's actions, the combination of choices he makes, are always functions of the values he holds. In other words, values determine choice. Consequently, to experience the quality of life desired requires selecting values appropriate to such a life.

The thing that is awry in the search for functional, abundant living is not usually desire, determination, or commitment. The failure lies in the area of values conflict; that is, trying to live the Christian life through actions undergirded by incompatible values. Not only does the appropriate set of values determine the right combination of choices, but it also brings energy into our lives. As Roy Posner in "The Power of Personal Values" states, "Values are expressions of emotionalized truths that when implemented energize whatever they come in contact with, enabling the greatest positive results." [12]

2. Values defined: According to Scott Williams in "Clarifying and Applying Personal Values: Priorities and Integrity" and the *American Heritage Dictionary,* "Value" carries the following meanings:

- A belief, a mission, or a philosophy that is meaningful
- Beliefs of a person or social group in which they have an emotional investment (either for or against something)
- Regard highly; esteem; rate according to relative estimate of worth or desirability.
- Consider or rate highly [13][14]

In a more technical sense, Roy Posner describes our values as "the formation and ideations of thought, the distinct formulations of understanding that express what we perceive to be important truths about life. These ideals are then reinforced by our emotions and feelings, which turn those mental perceptions into a vital passion that we hope to realize in our lives."[15]

Following is a definition or description of values that minimizes any confusion caused by some of the terms used to identify and to describe the term *values*; it also provides an indisputable way for one to determine which values provide the foundation of one's actions. Dr. Tony E. Roach in *You Are God's Love Bank* points out that our individual values are the personal goals we seek on a daily basis to meet our needs, desires, and wants; that is, our values are the "price tags" we place on what we believe is most important in our life—those things we esteem highly.[16]

3. The composition of values: Values have two basic components: (1) current beliefs, the rules that determine what we do each day; and (2) attitude, the temporary paradigm for carrying out our rules and the "eyeglasses" through which we view and assess the world around us. For example, if an individual identifies honesty as a value by which he lives but frequently takes deceptive measures to resolve potentially embarrassing situations or to gain an advantage over others, honesty is clearly not a real value of that person.

4. The power of values: The power of values lies in the fact that they control the lives we live on a daily basis. Obviously, when a force exercises such dominance in the quality of our lives, understanding that force is of paramount importance. It is only when we achieve such understanding that we are able to begin gaining control of our actions.

Dr. Roach lists four advantages a person gains when he understands his value system. They include the following: (a) identifying the beliefs that lead him to do what he does in his life, (b) developing the ability to set goals in life and to move toward those goals, (c) recognizing the factors that shape his paradigm, and (d) understanding the difference between living a life of abundant empowerment or a life of disempowerment. [17]

5. Values and change: Because of the role that values play in actual behavior, merely changing behavior proves to be ineffective. Even when the change in behavior is successful, all too often the new behavior does not last. Even if the particular original behavior does not recur, stimuli in an entirely different area will often produce similar dysfunctional behavior. Why does this happen?

The primary reason for this ineffective change is the failure to address the underlying basis of behavior—values. According to Dick Nelson in his article "Values and Behavior Change," values rather than behavior must be the target for permanent and lasting change. In other words, if a person wants to experience lasting change in his life, he must first experience change in his values rather than temporary change in his behavior. [18]

6. The source of values: However, even heavily emphasizing values is not sufficient for sustained change. One can choose from scores of values and with varying degrees of commitment and intensity. A vital issue involves which values to choose and the source of those values, as well as the whys of those particular values and how they can be successfully developed and incorporated into one's life. In other words, whose standard should be used in the formulation and reformation of values: God's or man's? Care must be taken to maintain awareness that the objective is not simply to live by good values, but to live by values anchored in and derived from God.

Values come from only one of two sources and rest on only one of two foundations. They are either the true values of heaven or the false values of the world. The behavior they produce will either be anchored in heaven or anchored in the world.

For all Christians, God's instructions are explicitly clear. The Holy Spirit's counsel is, "If then you have been raised up with Christ, keep seeking the things above, where Christ is, seated at the right hand of God. Set your mind on the things above, not on the things that are on earth" (Col. 3:1–2). In this verse, the verb phrase "keep seeking" means to look for, to seek out, to try to obtain, to desire to possess, and to strive for. While it is true that the Holy Spirit provides the power, the individual Christian must provide the desiring, the seeking, and the striving. Setting our desires on heavenly things is the goal that focuses our choices. This answers both the what and the source of the values Christians are to make their own.

When Christians experience a lack of consistency and harmony in daily living, conflicts in their values are the cause. Those conflicts lead to frustrations, and frustrations generally lead to the doing of dysfunctional things in order to cope; hence, a dysfunctional life results. On the other hand, when values are internally consistent, both within the individual and with the divine standard, Christians enjoy clarity, peace, oneness, and atonement with God, self, and significant others in their lives. In other words, they experience functional, abundant living. However, to consistently enjoy functional, abundant living, a Christian must (1) understand heaven's values, (2) clearly make heaven's values the most important values, and then (3) elect to bring the requisite level of energy to living by heaven's values.

Daily we are bombarded by words, ideas, images, and philosophies that teach and fortify the values of this world. Society is constantly teaching us that (1) intellectual prowess, (2) physical attractiveness, (3) material possessions, (4) worldly achievements, and (5) the approval of others are the things to value. However, God naturally has an entirely different view of what should form a person's value system.

Through the prophet Jeremiah, God said this: "Let not a wise man boast of his wisdom, and let not the mighty man boast of his might, let not a rich man boast of his riches; but let him who boasts boast of this, that he understands and knows Me, that I am the Lord who exercises lovingkindness, justice, and righteousness on earth; for I delight in these things" (Jer. 9:23–24). The New Living Translation gives a vivid and clear application of verse 24: "Let them boast in this alone: that they truly know me and understand that I am the Lord who is just and righteous, whose love is unfailing, and that I delight in these things. I, the Lord, have spoken!" In other words, God puts a higher priority on knowing Him personally and living a life that reflects His justice and His righteousness. Values that are thus focused are the things that the Lord says please Him.

Chapter 7

Change: God's Principles Versus Man's Theories (Part 2)

Jesus Is the Answer

God's answer to and His provisions for true, functional, abundant living is His Son, Jesus Christ. Through Jesus Christ, all life began, and in Him is all the best that God gives (John 1:4; 11:25; 14:6; Col. 1:17–18; 1 John 5:12).

1. Jesus models heaven's values: To counteract the false values of the world's system with which we have been bombarded from birth, we must first have a set of godly values to serve as value targets, value models, and value indicators to help us live the lives God has called us to live in this world. In "Values and Behavior Change," Dick Nelson states that values are gained and reformed largely through mimicking significant, credible, authoritative people.[19] Who is more significant, credible, and authoritative than Jesus Christ?

Jesus was the most successful person to ever live. As a means to ensure success in gaining and reforming our values, the Holy Spirit issues this command: "Have this attitude in yourselves which was also in Christ Jesus" (Phil. 2:5). "Have this attitude in yourselves" implies to think, to regard, to hold an opinion, or to set one's mind on something. In this verse, the command, then, is to think like Christ Jesus. Our opinions are to mirror His opinions; our minds are to be set on the same things as His mind; our affections, our consciences, are to be as His. As this happens, the mind, or attitude, of the Lord Jesus Christ becomes ours and thus becomes the paradigm, or eyeglasses, through which we see life and its many demands.

According to 2 Corinthians 3:18, one of the ministries of the Holy Spirit is to transform us into the image, or likeness, of Christ Jesus. Furthermore, we are told that Jesus left an example for us to "follow in His steps" (1 Pet. 2:21). Therefore, it is the life of Jesus that God uses as His outline sketch to shape our lives, to instill and reform our values. As we understand and internalize the beliefs and the attitude of Jesus, as we make them our beliefs and attitude, we cooperate with the Holy Spirit in His ministry of transforming us into the image of Jesus. As we do so, we are able to achieve the same results in our living that Jesus achieved in His.

2. We are to mimic Jesus' values: The significant, credible, and authoritative person whose values we are to adopt is the Lord Jesus Christ. Jesus Christ serves as our value target, value model, and value indicator. As our value target, Jesus' life and teachings serve as an objective to aim for in making our combinations of choices; that is, from Him we receive the correct data by which to develop the right values. As our value model, Jesus' actions become our focus in daily decision making; that is, mimicking the life of Jesus reforms our world-based values. As our value indicator, Jesus' life helps us to visualize living as He lived, thus providing indication to us and others that we are making the correct combination of choices that produce functional, abundant living.

When we carefully examine the dissatisfaction many Christians often experience in their attempts to live functional, abundant lives, the cause can usually be traced to one or all of the world's false core values of intellectual prowess, physical attractiveness, material possessions, worldly achievements, or the approval of others. However, the more we internalize the values of Jesus, the more deeply His values actually become our own. As an outgrowth of this internalization of values, we begin to focus less on the false values of intelligence and human wisdom and more on the true value of atonement in our single most important relationship with God. We focus less on the false values of physical attractiveness and human might and more on the true value of God's steadfast love, experiencing God's love for ourselves and showing it to others. We become less occupied with the love of the things of this world and more concerned with God's righteousness and justice, and we use His righteousness and justice to live the lives the Lord Jesus died to give us.

3. The main thing: In some manner, each Christian must answer several key questions about his life. These questions include the following: "What are the truths of my life?" "What ideals and beliefs have shaped my life?" "What ideals and beliefs are motivating and driving my life today?"[20] From the answers to these or similar questions, he can then begin to determine how each factor has, or currently is, shaping his life. Clarification of values can occur in no other way.

Jesus taught that the most important thing in Christians' lives is—and must be—God and their relationship with Him. He taught, "You shall love the Lord your God with all your heart and with all your soul and with all your mind. This is the great and foremost commandment" (Matt. 22:37–38). The apostle Paul, perhaps the most successful proponent of New Testament Christianity the world has ever known (other than Jesus Christ), was successful because he was committed to keeping the main thing in his life the main thing. To the Philippian church, he identified the main thing when he wrote, "I count all things to be loss in view of the surpassing value of knowing Christ Jesus my Lord" (Phil. 3:8).

The Holy Spirit teaches that one's relationship with God is what man was created for and what his existence is all about (Eccles. 12:13; Rev. 4:11). Each Christian must determine the price tag he places on his relationship with God. All the rest of heaven's values are built on this foundational value.

There is a very interesting observation that can be made about the formation and reformation of values. Although the combination of choices we make is indeed influenced by our values, those choices also influence our values over time. Simply stated, when we choose to act like Jesus over an extended period of time, our values begin to change to conform to His values. In other words, His values eventually become our values.

For example, an individual Christian might not actually possess Jesus' values but does possess the desire to please God; so, in spite of the fact that he does not really want to accept the choices that should be made, he makes them anyway. As he does so consistently over a period of time, the Holy Spirit, little by little, uses his actions to form in him values consistent with the appropriate choices he is making. This fact points out the importance of commandment-based living instead of feeling-based living. Obeying God's commands, even when one does not feel like doing so, gradually produces the value that in turn produces the desire.

Chapter 8

Change: God's Principles Versus Man's Theories (Part 3)

Divinely Sourced Values

Remember, the objective is not just to make us good citizens, good workers, or good persons, for good citizens, good workers, and good people have existed throughout history. Rather, the objective is to make us Christlike in worship, character, and service. Through studying the life and lessons of Jesus as He ministered on earth, we gain a good sense of the core values by which He lived His life, the core values that made Him the most successful person to have ever lived.

Jesus' life and teachings cover the entire array of human needs, desires, and wants, and every spiritual principle He taught may be found in His parables. The values Jesus taught and lived by are termed "divinely sourced values" because the extent to which these values must be exercised and the reasons for living by them are anchored in God's requirements for kingdom living; they are, therefore, products of divine, not human, wisdom. Totally living by these values requires complete surrender to an authority higher than human authority, a feat beyond human capability. Consequently, not only were these values created by God (Eph. 2:10), they are also empowered by God (Phil. 2:13; Eph. 3:16, 20; Ezek. 36:27). In short, divinely sourced values are values based on God's principles for functional, abundant living, and they are energized by God's Spirit. Listed below are several divinely sourced values that we will examine:

1. Divinely sourced honesty: This value could be defined as integrity in all relationships in life, beginning with our relationship with God, which affects every other relationship in life, including our relationship with ourselves. [21]

A key factor in this value deals not only with integrity itself but also with the recognition of how the setting of priorities affects relationships; specifically, how the placing of top priority on integrity in one's relationship with God has a correlative effect on integrity in all other relationships in life.

In His life and teachings, Jesus clearly demonstrated the importance of relationships, integrity in those relationships, and the most important of all relationships: one's relationship with God. Responding to the question of which is the foremost commandment, Jesus said, "You shall love the Lord your God with all your heart, and with all your soul, and with your entire mind. This is the great and foremost commandment. The second is like it. You shall love your neighbor as yourself. On these two commandments depend the whole Law and the Prophets" (Matt. 22:37–40). Therefore, this value functions to develop and maintain truthfulness in all relationships, beginning with one's relationship with God. It recognizes the fact that all one's relationships are never as stable as they can be unless integrity in one's relationship with God is as it should be.

This value is seen in Jesus' combination of choices and resultant actions during His wilderness struggles as recorded in the Synoptic Gospels (Matt. 4:1–11; Mark 1:12–13; Luke 4:1–13). This event clearly shows that although Jesus was God in human flesh, He was vulnerable to the same temptations that humans throughout history have faced. In various encounters with Satan throughout His life, Jesus had to deal with the age-old human temptations common to all: the satisfaction of fleshly appetites, the urge to have what is pleasing to the eye, and the desire to give vent to pride (see Gen. 3:1–8).

It should be noted, Jesus made His combination of choices following a forty-day fast. The narrative states that following His fast, "He, then, became hungry" (Matt. 4:2; Luke 4:2). In other words, His need for nourishment acutely came back into focus. The question, then, is not whether Jesus needed food; with His life in jeopardy and His needing—not just desiring—food, the question becomes, how would Jesus get the food He needed to satisfy His human hunger? Satan presented Him with three choices, choices to satisfy not only human hunger but also to satisfy the desires to please the eye and to give vent to pride. Nevertheless, each choice Jesus made reflected integrity in His relationship with God and with Himself.

First, Jesus showed integrity in his fidelity to God's Word: "It is written, 'Man shall not live on bread alone, but on every word that proceeds out of the mouth of God'" (Matt. 4:4; Luke 4:4). Second, He showed integrity in His dependency on God's providential care: "It is written, 'You shall not put the Lord your God to the test' " (Matt. 4:7; Luke 4:12). Third, He showed integrity in His worship of God: "Begone, Satan! For it is written, 'You shall worship the Lord your God, and serve Him only' " (Matt. 4:10; Luke 4:8). Jesus' divinely sourced integrity revealed that God could depend on Him. How much integrity would Jesus have shown in His relationship with God if He, regardless of provocations, would have yielded to the temptations that characterize the things of the world rather than the things of heaven (1 John 2:15–17)?

Jesus' success did not depend on supernatural power. His desire to be honest in His relationship with God produced His specific combination of choices—actions learned through the things He encountered in life (Heb. 5:8). An element that must not be overlooked is the fact that Jesus' responses were directly related to God's Word and His fidelity to God's Word. In each instance, Jesus' response to Satan was, "It is written."

In similar fashion, a Christian must be extremely clear concerning what He believes about God, about the all-sufficiency of God's Word to address all human problems, and about the ministry of the indwelling Holy Spirit to empower God's Word in his life. Unless there is firm belief in these, he will be reluctant to rely solely on principles contained in the Bible and more apt to rely on principles gleaned from other sources.

After Jesus made His combination of choices that resulted in maintaining His integrity in His relationship with God, the narrative states, "Angels came and began to minister to Him" (Matt. 4:11). God always honor our integrity.

Living by the same value of divinely sourced integrity will lead us to adopt the same strategy of defense that Jesus used and will thus lead us to be honest in our relationship with God, with ourselves, and with others.

2. Divinely Sourced Courage: As a value, courage encompasses the ability and the willingness to remain faithful to the standard of right and wrong based on the Word of God even when the popular opinion encourages otherwise. It means to remain faithful even if such faithfulness results in pain, suffering, abandonment by family or friends, or standing alone. It is characterized by the knowing that God's standard of right and wrong is always best in any situation. [22]

More and more in the society in which Christians are called to live, the pressures to compromise God's standard in order to be politically correct and to accept and honor humanistic theories such as pluralism and relativism are increasing dramatically. Likewise, even among the community of the Lord's disciples, the pressures to conform to the larger society are increasing dramatically. As a result, many like to think that no age has had to cope with the complexities of living that we face today.

Interestingly, however, Jesus was confronted with the same kinds of pressures to compromise what He believed was right according to God's standard. Although not every one of Jesus' temptations or trials is recorded in the four gospels, what is recorded is a series of temptations representative of the temptations faced by humans today. In each of them, Jesus demonstrated His divinely sourced courage.

When one considers the life of Jesus and the courage He displayed, the one act that usually stands above all others was His willingness to face the cross and crucifixion. That is as it should be because the cross was an act of extreme courage. However, all of Jesus' life reflected the epitome of divinely sourced courage, the ability to remain faithful to the standard of right and wrong as defined by God. Many times He was confronted with situations where compromise would have been the easiest and safest course to take; yet in each situation, His combination of choices demonstrated His divinely sourced courage.

Throughout Jesus' ministry, He exposed the self-righteousness and arrogance, the hypocrisy and unfaithfulness, of the Jewish religious elite. His denunciations recorded in Matthew 23:1–36 are classic examples, and several of His parables display this same group of people in a very unflattering light. For example, knowing the antipathy in which His fellow countrymen held Samaritans, Jesus made a despised Samaritan the hero, and a priest and a Levite the insensitive ones, in the notable parable of Luke 10:30–37. In the parable of Luke 18:9–14, He compared the actions of a despised sinner to the actions of a Pharisee and declared the sinner more justified. Similarly, He declared a sinful woman's actions as more righteous than the actions of a self-righteous Pharisee (Luke 7:36–50; for more examples, see also Matt. 21:28–32; Luke 10:30–37; 18:9–14).

Not only did Jesus denounce the Jewish religious elite in scathing terms, but He also denounced the Jewish nation for its unfaithfulness as God's covenant people (see Luke 3:1–9; 14:16–24; 20:9–18). In Luke 19:45–48, He is seen upsetting the economic well-being of the established order as He drove from the temple courts those who profaned the sanctity of the temple and its worship by selling cattle, sheep, and doves, and by changing money. The Bible reveals several incidents in which Jesus relieved human suffering by healing on the Sabbath and thereby incurred the anger of the religious elite (Luke 13:10–17; 14:1–6).

Was Jesus surprised or caught off guard by the extremely negative reactions of others to His acts and teachings? If so, then His acts that appear as courageous may be dismissed as nothing more than good intentions that resulted in unanticipated reactions. The Bible, however, teaches in several places that Jesus possessed profound insight into human nature (Matt. 89:4; 12:25; Luke 6:8; 9:47; 11:17; John 2:24–25). Therefore, the reactions to Him and His teaching came as no surprise to Him. He knew that He and His teachings would be rejected, and He knew the hostility that He would incur.

But despite the unpopularity of His teachings, and despite the personal risk and cost attached to them, Jesus knew what the Father wanted Him to do and teach, and those were the things He did and taught. How was He able to demonstrate such courage? In John 8:28 and 5:19, Jesus attributed all that He was able to do in life to His being sent by the Father and to His connection with the Father. His courage was courage anchored in the Father.

Furthermore, it is imperative to keep in mind that although He was divine, Jesus was also fully human. The quality of life He lived was not the result of supernatural power, but the combination of choices made. True, He was the one and only Son of God; however, it was through life's challenges that He learned faithfulness to the Father (Heb. 5:8). He was subjected to the same trials and temptations as we are, yet His combination of choices produced sinless living (Heb. 4:15). Even though He knew persecution and death (death on a cross was, by any measure, a horrible way to die) awaited Him in Jerusalem, "He resolutely set His face [He made up His mind firmly] to go to Jerusalem" (Luke 9:51). Divinely sourced courage freed Jesus from the manipulation that would have resulted from preoccupation with the opinions of the Jewish religious elite and others, and it positioned Him to give precedence to what honored God. Living by divinely sourced courage, we, too, will experience the same success.

3. Divinely sourced forgiveness: This is the ability to accept and to allow God's concept of forgiveness to work in our lives and in our relationships, recognizing that forgiveness as God designed it and as He empowers us to practice it sets us free from the negative feelings and emotions attached to wrongs suffered. Forgiveness releases both the offender and the one offended, setting both free. [23]

When God created Adam, He declared, "It is not good for the man to be alone" (Gen. 2:18). With this declaration, God asserted man's creation as a social being. To meet the man's need for suitable companionship, God created woman and brought her to the man (Gen. 2:21–22). In so doing, God formed the first interpersonal relationship. Such interpersonal relations are crucial to the functioning of the human community.

Full appreciation of the value of forgiveness requires an appreciation of its nature and its power. Divine forgiveness is a hallmark of the Christian faith (Luke 24:46–47); it is woven into the very fabric of God's grace (2 Cor. 8:9; Eph. 1:6–7). Divine forgiveness is as necessary to functional, abundant living as oxygen is to physical life; we need it, and God freely and liberally provides it. Nonetheless, many Christians suffer dysfunctional lives because of the lack of this vital value.

Christians fail to benefit fully from living as God's community and living in God's community because of dysfunctional relationships in their lives resulting from their failure to forgive. Even among those who ardently practice forgiveness, many still struggle with relationships suffering from past hurts and wrongs. Why does this occur? It is not that these individuals deliberately set out to have dysfunctional relationships; rather, it is that many of them have bought into this world's concept of forgiveness, which is based on human wisdom. But divinely sourced forgiveness is by its very nature based on God's wisdom and is possible only when one accepts God's concept of forgiveness.

In Matthew 18:23–33, Jesus gave an easily understood example of God's concept of forgiveness, the kind of forgiveness necessary to kingdom living. Verses 15–20 contain Jesus' teaching concerning the handling of offenses between those in covenant relationship with God who have been wronged by another or who have wronged another. The parable related in verses 23–34 was prompted by Peter's question, how often must one forgive another? "Up to seven times?" he asked (v. 21). Peter's question deals with the issue of quantity and suggests that there is a limit to forgiveness beyond which one is not required to go.

Jesus, however, responded to the quantity issue with these words: "I do not say to you, up to seven times, but up to seventy times seven" (v. 22). The application, therefore, is that forgiveness has no limit. God's concept of forgiveness deals not with numbers, but rather with the requirement to extend forgiveness as long as there is a need to forgive.

There are three situations in which divinely sourced forgiveness is required and where it must be displayed: (1) when a person requests forgiveness (Luke 17:3–4); (2) when a Christian has knowledge that another has something against him (Matt. 5:23–24); and (3) when a Christian has something against another person (Mark 11:25). As long as any of these conditions exist, forgiveness is mandated.

To address the issue of quality and to provide a clear example of God's concept of forgiveness, Jesus taught a parable in verses 23–33 about a servant who had been shown extraordinary mercy by his master but who in turn refused to show the same quality of mercy to one who owed him a debt. Four times in this passage (vv. 21, 27, 32, and also in v. 35), Jesus used the Greek verb "aphiemi" which is translated "to forgive" in English. This Greek word carries the meanings of "to send away," "to dismiss," "to remove," "to let go of," "to give up," and "to send forth." The application is to send away the wrong done, to remove it as an item in the relationship, to dismiss it from the offender. A concrete example of the action this word requires in found in Psalm 103:12, where in speaking of God's concept of forgiveness, the psalmist says, "As far as the east is from the west, so has He [God] removed our transgressions from us." In other words, once forgiven, our sins against God never arise again in our relationship with Him (Jer. 31:34).

In verse 35, Jesus provided the application: "So shall My heavenly Father also do to you [that is, not grant mercy to those who do not grant to mercy to others], if each of you does not forgive his brother from your heart." Forgiveness from the heart carries the idea of complete forgiveness, forgiveness in deed and in truth. Forgiveness from the heart becomes easier when a person considers the fact that nothing another has done to him remotely compares to what he has done to God. Yet God freely and completely forgives us and thus demands that we freely and completely forgive others. The fact is, without divinely sourced forgiveness, a person simply cannot be fully content, effective, and happy in his relationships with others, with himself, or with God.

Jesus taught the singular, extraordinary, uncommon expression of divinely sourced forgiveness as He hung dying on the cross. His life oozing away with every struggling breath, suffering unimaginable agony and enduring the torment of those watching Him die, He did not call for vengeance upon His tormenters. Instead, His prayer was, "Father, forgive them; for they do not know what they are doing" (Luke 23:43). Not only is it true that only God could die like that, but it is equally true that only God can forgive like that. And this is the quality of forgiveness God requires of us.

Ephesians 4:32 says, "And be kind to one another, tender-hearted, forgiving each other, just as God in Christ also has forgiven you" (see also Col. 3:13). In God's concept of forgiveness, the focus is not on self, but on others. Relationship is valued over personal hurts; thus, forgiveness takes the initiative in the restoration of relationships. It reflects the mind and the actions of Christ Himself.

The most common New Testament meaning of this concept of forgiveness,"charizomai", carries the idea of graciously remitting a person's wrongs. It is considered divinely sourced because only God can forgive like that, and only those that God empowers can forgive like that. As we Christians become more and more governed by the Holy Spirit of God, the value of divinely sourced forgiveness becomes more of a reality in our relationships, and our relationships reflect more of what God intended when He created us in His image and brought us together as social beings.

4. Divinely sourced power: This value enables us to exercise our God-given ability to choose our own responses to the circumstances with which we are confronted in life. It means being proactive rather than reactive, knowing that how we respond to those circumstances determines the quality of life we live, and realizing that God has empowered us with the ability to always respond in a manner that honors Him. [24]

One of the unfortunate facts of life is that many Christians spend the greater part of their lives longing for, regretting not having, or envying those who have the power that comes from wealth, political position, fame, great beauty, or advanced education. They believe their lives would indeed be more enjoyable, more worthwhile, more profitable, and of a higher quality if only they had such power. However, they fail to effectively realize that all lives are replete with choices, those choices determine decisions, and those decisions produce results that determine the true quality of life. But most important of all, such Christians fail to accept what Jesus teaches about life, its quality, and the proper place of material things.

Jesus taught that all the trappings of worldly power do not add real quality to life. He warned, "Beware, and be on your guard against every form of greed; for not even when one has an abundance does his life consist of his possessions" (Luke 12:15). In fact, the Preacher in Ecclesiastes concluded that all of it—wisdom, pleasure, human achievements, and great riches—was "vanity and striving after wind" (12:11). When all is said and done, it means nothing.

Sadder still is that while longing for the power they do not have, these same Christians neglect the real power they and all Christians have to make their lives more enjoyable, more worthwhile, more profitable, and of a higher quality. What is this power each Christian possesses? It is the power to choose our responses to life and its many diverse circumstances. The importance of such power is seen when we realize that life is 10 percent what happens to us and 90 percent how we react to it.

A cardinal fact of creation is that God gave humans the power to choose. A main message we glean from Adam and Eve is that although God gives us the power to choose, He also holds us responsible for our choices. God does not force us to make the choices He knows are best; rather, He allows us to exercise our power of choice.

However, the other side of the freedom-of-choice coin is the consequences of those choices. Generally, the true quality of life experienced is the result of our choices. Though not forcing us to choose in a certain way, God does provide us with the right information to guide us in selecting the choices we make. He gives us His written Word and the indwelling of His Holy Spirit to help us understand His Word and to empower us in obeying it.

The importance of having the right source of information upon which to base a choice is graphically illustrated by Jesus in His wilderness temptation in Matthew 4. Jesus had to use His power to choose between being self-reliant or dependent on God (v. 1), to select a method to accomplish an end (vv. 5–6), and to determine a way to gain power and influence (vv. 8–9). In each instance, His choice was guided by God's Word; and in each instance, Jesus made His choice based on what was written there. Each time, He said, "It is written" (vv. 4, 7, 10).

Every day He lived on this earth, Jesus used His divinely sourced power to choose responses that honored God (John 8:29). And just like Jesus, we face scores of opportunities to exercise this power of choice every day of our lives. Every time we exercise the power of choice, we actively choose the path we travel, the quality of life we live, the success or failure of our endeavors, and even our destination and destiny. Each time, we choose to exercise either the power granted through our natural abilities or the power that is divinely sourced.

In concluding the parable of the rich farmer (Luke 12:16–20), Jesus, having already declared that possessions do not make for true quality living, pointed to the only riches that really matter. In verse 21, He said, "So is the man who lays up treasure for himself, and is not rich toward God." In concluding his personal discovery of the futility of the acquisition of power, possessions, and popularity, the Preacher asserted that the only thing in life that really matters is one's relationship with God (Eccles. 12:13–14). And from the prophet Jeremiah, we read, "Thus says the Lord, 'Let not a wise man boast of his wisdom, and let not the mighty man boast of his might, let not a rich man boast of his riches; but let him who boasts boast of this, that he understands and knows Me, that I am the Lord who exercises lovingkindness, justice, and righteousness on earth; for I delight in these things,' declares the Lord" (Jer. 9:23–24).

The components of Jesus' success were not earthly power, companions, popularity, or favorable circumstances. Jesus utilized His divinely sourced power to choose His responses to the events happening to Him. In all situations, He chose to respond in a manner that maintained integrity to His ministry, God's purpose, and His goal. Every choice He made carried Him toward the ultimate goal for which He came to the earth.

The decisions and choices we make determine the true quality of the lives we live; therefore, instead of using our ability to choose the things this world teaches are important, we are better served by exercising our divinely sourced power to make choices that bring abundant living into reality.

True, we are going to face difficult conditions in practically every aspect of society. But regardless of how much worldly power others have, how unfairly those with power exercise it, or how messed up things are, we can enjoy functional, abundant living. We can exercise our divinely sourced power to choose the life to which God has called us, the life Christ died for us to have. Choosing to honor God is the right choice in any and all circumstances, and God always honors those who honor Him (Ps. 91:15; John 12:26).

Chapter 9

Change: God's Principles Versus Man's Theories (Part 4)

Divinely Sourced Values (Continued)

5. **Divinely sourced purpose:** This value is the effective recognition that God has a purpose for everything He created and that we have the capacity to seek that purpose in our daily lives. Living by God's purpose enables us to experience the good that God is able to bring out of all circumstances in our lives.[25]

The definition of *purpose* as listed in the *American Heritage Dictionary*, *Brown-Driver-Briggs Hebrew Dictionary* of Old Testament Words, and *Thayer's Greek Definitions* of New Testament Words, is "to plan and design." Purpose speaks to the goal toward which one strives or the reason for which something exists. In the context of this value and the teachings of Scripture, God's purpose speaks of why God did what He did, why God is doing what He is doing, and why God will do what He has promised to do. Included in this is the role God designated to each person

He placed on this planet; that is, why God gave life to each of us.

In Ephesians 3:8–11, the Bible speaks of God's "eternal purpose . . . carried out in Christ Jesus." The question is, what has God carried out in Christ that is eternal in nature? Second Corinthians 5:18–19 states that God was in Christ "reconciling the world to Himself." This action was not an afterthought, as some teach; this purpose of reconciliation in Christ was set before the world was created.

God describes His creation as good (Gen. 1:10, 12, 17, 21, 25) and very good (v. 31); however, through the influence of Satan, God's good creation was spoiled. In God, eternal purpose is the action of reversing, through Jesus Christ, the sin damage caused by Adam and Eve (Genesis 3). Ultimately, it is to create a people for His possession who are "holy and blameless before Him in love" (Eph. 1:4).

Within this context, Romans 8:28 is more easily understood: "And we know that God causes all things to work together for good to those who love God, to those who are called according to His purpose." Because God's purpose is to make us like His Son (Rom. 8:29; 2 Cor. 3:18), it involves those things that make us like Jesus; that is, those things that work to promote true welfare, devotion to God, and a life of true peace and happiness. So then, the career that one has, the many friends by which one is surrounded, the health with which one has been blessed, the education that one has acquired, all the opportunities that come one's way, all fit the definition of "good," in the context of this verse, if they make us more like Jesus and thereby prepare us to live with God in heaven. In this context, we are able to fully understand such statements of Jesus as, "My food is to do the work of Him who sent Me" (John 4:34); ". . . having accomplished the work" that God gave Him (John 17:4); and "for this purpose [death on a cross] I came to this hour" (John 12:27).

In the parable of the fig tree in Luke 13:6–9, Jesus painted a vivid picture of the dangers involved in not living up to the purpose for which one exists:

> And He began telling this parable: "A man had a fig tree which had been planted in his vineyard; and he came looking for fruit on it and did not find any. And he said to the vineyard-keeper, 'Behold, for three years I have come looking for fruit on this fig tree without finding any. Cut it down! Why does it even use up the ground?'
>
> "And he answered and said to him, 'Let it alone, sir, for this year too, until I dig around it and put in fertilizer; and if it bears fruit next year, fine; but if not, cut it down.' "

Jesus' expectation regarding another fig tree is quite instructive. In the narrative found in Mark 11:11–14, we read:

> Jesus entered Jerusalem and came into the temple; and after looking around at everything, He left for Bethany with the twelve, since it was already late. On the next day, when they had left Bethany, He became hungry. Seeing at a distance a fig tree in leaf, He went to see if perhaps He would find anything on it; and when He came to it, He found nothing but leaves, for it was not the season for figs. He said to it, "May no one ever eat fruit from you again!" And His disciples were listening.

In this instance, Jesus approached a fig tree in full leaf, expecting to find fruit. He did not go to a palm tree and expect to find figs there. The reason is quite plain: palm trees are not designed to produce figs. The purpose of the fig tree is to produce figs. Only when it is producing figs is the fig tree enjoying its full potential and producing the good it was designed to produce.

One of Satan's tactics is to paralyze Christians as they try to determine their God-given purpose or to convince them to delay involvement in any ministry until they have discovered their true purpose. In such cases, Satan successfully turns a good thing, knowing and fulfilling one's purpose, into a bad thing. However, the strategy to overcome him in this effort is really quite simple: imitate the purpose fulfillment of God.

Three specific attributes are always present in God's purpose, and by focusing one's actions around these attributes while seeking to fulfill God's purpose, the aim of purpose fulfillment can be achieved. What are these three attributes? According to Romans 9:17–24, these attributes are as follows: (1) to show God's power, (2) to proclaim God's name, and (3) to make known God's glory. When a Christian has these attributes as the basis for what he does, he is, in fact, living true to the reason for his existence. He is living by the value of divinely sourced purpose and is enjoying all the good God has placed in his life (1 Tim. 6:17; James 1:17).

6. Divinely sourced excellence: This value may be characterized as the faith required to look beyond the seen to the unseen, to confront the conditions of life with the expectation that all can be overcome. It is knowing that God's exceedingly great power is greater than any situation with which we are faced. [26]

There are two intertwined key concepts in self-excellence: (1) faith and (2) the impact of faith on one's ability to achieve. Faith may be anchored in many objects and works on many different levels with varying degrees of strength. Faith in one's abilities, faith in one's physician, and faith in the safety of air travel are but a few examples. In each case, the quality of the faith determines the effort expended relative to the object of faith and thereby determines the outcome. Strong faith produces strong, effective action, which in turn leads to successful outcomes.

However, faith that is 100 percent effective 100 percent of the time in 100 percent of situations is faith anchored securely in God. When true faith in God is present, two specific elements are evident: (1) trust in and reliance on God and (2) faithfulness to God in everyday living. When such faith exists in one's life at a high level, one is then able to "see the invisible, believe the incredible, and receive the impossible."[27]

Dealing with the many and varied situations of life is seldom as simple as having no faith at all or having an abundance of faith. In reality, our faith lies somewhere between the two extremes, much like the father of Mark 9:17–27. In this passage of Scripture, a father brought his son, who was possessed with an evil spirit, to Jesus (v. 17). This spirit caused the son to do destructive things to himself (v. 18). Jesus' disciples had tried to cast out the spirit but had failed, so in response to his son's plight, the father begged Jesus, "But if you can do anything, take pity on us and help us!" (v. 22). These words reveal the father's doubts and his admission of the possibility that maybe Jesus, like the disciples, could not cast out the spirit.

In response, Jesus said to him, "If you can! All things are possible to him who believes" (v. 23). Obviously, this man did not have overcoming faith. But neither was his condition a situation of no faith. Notice, now, his response to Jesus: "I do believe; help my unbelief." In other words, he was saying, "Lord, I do believe, but I need You to bring aid to my nagging doubts" (v. 24). In his request, the father simply asked Jesus for the faith to see and expect what he on his own could neither see nor expect: the inconceivable and the incredible. This father lacked the excellence of faith, but he understood that and petitioned Jesus for what he himself did not possess. Consequently, what he could not see at first, he became able to see; what he could not conceive as possible at first, he soon realized: the healing of his son.

A very familiar example of this concept of excellence in faith is that of Abraham as recorded in Romans 4. Notice the role Abraham's faith played in his accomplishments in God's eternal purpose.

> When God promised Abraham that he would become the father of many nations, Abraham believed him. God had also said, "Your descendants will be as numerous as the stars," even though such a promise seemed utterly impossible! And Abraham's faith did not weaken, even though he knew that he was too old to be a father at the age of one hundred and that Sarah, his wife, had never been able to have children. Abraham never wavered in believing God's promise. In fact, his faith grew stronger, and in this he brought glory to God. He was absolutely convinced that God was able to do anything he promised.
> —Romans 4:18–20, NLT

Because of his excellence of faith, Abraham—although marked by failure—became all that God had built into him. Furthermore, he was given the singular distinction of being called the friend of God (James 2:23).

If it were possible to live out our faith in words only and only within the confines of worship services and Bible classes, almost universal excellence of faith would exist among the Lord's people. Excellence of faith among us would be the rule and not the exception. However, faith exists not merely in words but also in actions; the quality of the actions reflects the quality, or excellence, of the faith from which the actions spring.

Many Christians excel in their faith when circumstances are perking along just right, but we all know that the circumstances of life do not always perk along just right. However, those not-just-right times are the most profitable in terms of quality living. An anonymous author wrote, "Faith is idle when circumstances are right; only when they are adverse is one's faith in God exercised. Faith, like muscle, grows strong and supple with exercise." Consequently, it is in the not-just-right times when the excellence of faith is developed.

Excellence simply means the state, quality, or condition of excelling. In other words, excellence is to do or be better than; it means to surpass, to be, or to go beyond a limit or standard. Excellence of faith is the quality of faith that is better than the average; it goes beyond mere expectations and exceeds the standard of mediocrity. Excellence of faith is always better than circumstances, conditions, limitations, and difficulties. It is the quality of faith that does the right thing regardless of the consequences, knowing that God will ultimately turn the efforts to good. When a person is living by excellence of faith, he expects the best from life in full measure. His faith is not the type that wishes, hopes, or desires; rather, it is a faith that receives.

What we accomplish in life depends on what we believe and how strongly those beliefs are held. That being true, the quality of our faith determines the quality of our approach to and living of life. This core value produced in Jesus the ability to accomplish what the Father sent Him to do. The fact is, to live the lives God has called us to live, to accomplish the purposes for which He gave us life, and to achieve the excellence that He wills, divinely sourced excellence must be the hallmark of our faith as well. Such faith is able to accomplish those things, not merely as the result of the possessor having it, but also because of the power inherent in it, "knowing that God is able to do exceeding abundantly above all that I ask or think, according to the power of the Holy Spirit working inside" (Eph. 3:20).

Divinely sourced excellence sees and claims the promises of God, and it makes those promises a present reality and a stimulus for great motives. Divinely sourced excellence lays hold of what is future and sure and brings it into the life of the possessor so that he lives and walks in both the presence and the power of faith. Such is the visualization of the Holy Spirit's teaching in 2 Corinthians 5:7: "For we walk [live] by faith and not by sight."

This, of course, becomes a reality only as one makes and continues to make the right evaluation of things; that is, when one takes the long view of 2 Corinthians 4:13–18. A question each Christian should ask himself is, does my faith expect the same ol' same ol', or am I living by the value of divinely sourced excellence and thus expecting the unexpected? In short, each of us must examine the kind of results our faith is producing in our lives.

7. Divinely sourced self-image: This value centers on the knowledge that we are created in God's image, a product of His divine workmanship, loved and valued by Him, which thus gives us the ability to reject the world's attempts to define us.[28]

What is self-image? For the sake of simplicity, I have eliminated the technical differences among self-concept, self-image, and self-esteem. Self-concept and self-image involve the thoughts, attitudes, and feelings people have about themselves; for example, their character traits, strengths, weaknesses, and physical features. Self-esteem, however, refers to the evaluation that people make of their worth, competence, and significance. Self-image and self-concept involve a self-description, whereas self-esteem involves a self-evaluation. Self-esteem encompasses the way people describe and evaluate themselves in relation to others and the feelings and perspective people have of themselves in relation to others. These descriptions, evaluations, and feelings determine how a person responds to the many and various requirements of life.

Jesus' parable of the talents as recorded in Matthew 25:14–30 provides an excellent example of the results of an ineffective self-image. In this parable, a wealthy man entrusted a specific sum of money to three of his slaves prior to leaving on a trip (vv. 14–15). To one, he gave five talents; to another, two talents; and to the other, one talent. The distribution was not arbitrary; he gave according to each man's ability (v. 15). Unfortunately and tragically, however, not all of the slaves rose to the challenge.

The slaves given the five and two talents doubled their value (vv. 16–17), and each received commendation from their master: "Well done, good and faithful slave. . . . Enter the joy of your master" (vv. 21, 23). On the other hand, the slave given only one talent "dug in the ground and hid his master's money" (v. 18), for which his master labeled him a "wicked, lazy slave" (v. 26). Why did this slave act as he did? In verse 24, the third slave reveals his perspective of his master in these words: "Master, I knew you to be a hard man, reaping where you did not sow, and gathering where you scattered no seed." As interesting as that observation may be, the slave's self-perspective is perhaps even more revealing.

This slave falsely believed he lacked the knowledge, skills, and ability to meet the master's challenge. How do we know this? It is obvious by what he felt and what he did! "I was afraid [terrified]," he stated (v. 25). Because of his low self-image, he took what he perceived as the route of no risk, no danger, and no failure: he hid the money. Tragically, the views he held of both his master and himself resulted in severe punishment (vv. 28–30).

The struggle to acquire and maintain an acceptable self-image is probably a universal struggle. At some point in life, all of us (some more than others) struggle with feelings of inferiority and low self-image resulting from the importance we attach to what others say to and about us and the weight we give to how others treat us. Unfortunately, many people mentally carry in their heads the results of these assumptions, and those results almost always influence how they think, feel, and act, both toward themselves and toward others.

Divinely sourced self-image is premised on the fact that a departure from the teachings of the Bible regarding the value of the individual is at the root of all problems of low self-image. When Adam and Eve first sinned, the self-image with which God created them was polluted. Ever since then, their offspring have been defining their self-image based on human wisdom instead of God's wisdom. Circumstances, life, other people, and self can be viewed correctly, and thus responded to effectively, only when viewed from the perspective of the one who created us, the source from whom all life comes and the one who has authority over everyone and everything—the almighty God.

In the Bible, God teaches about both Himself and ourselves. God confirms that we are created in His image, are valuable in His sight, and are the objects of His perfect love. Proving our innate worth, God sent His Son to pay for our sins, and to make possible our redemption and the renewal of communication with Him. He sent His Holy Spirit to guide us, angels to guard us, and the Bible to teach us. He made us Christians to be lights in the world, and He put us on cosmic display, shining forth His grace and wisdom.

The wisdom of this world, however, values the skills we exhibit, the abilities we exercise, the knowledge we possess, the things we accumulate, the people we know, the good we demonstrate, and the adulation we receive—all of which are fickle and fleeting. These, we are taught, are the things that create a positive self-image. Divinely sourced self-image, on the other hand, is anchored in God's Word, God's perspective, God's feelings, and God's actions. These are unchangeable and permanent. With a divinely sourced self-image, one does not need to compromise one's moral code to enhance pleasure, power, prestige, or privilege.

It does not matter how dysfunctional, damaging, and destructive a self-image a person possesses; accepting what God has revealed will make it right. The counsel of God is able to restore one's self-image to what God designed it to be in the first place (Ps. 19:7). Divinely sourced self-image reasons that a person will always arrive at the appropriate self-description when he esteems God's Word and actions toward him more highly than he esteems those of others. When a person consistently (1) listens to God though His written Word, (2) yields to the dictates of the Holy Spirit, and (3) makes the right application of the things of God in daily living, divinely sourced self-image is formed, and this image brings peace, pleasure, and prosperity (Ps. 1:1–6).

8. Divinely sourced discipline: This speaks of the ability to do the things that need to be done, when they need to be done, even when we do not want to do them or when doing them is painful. It is knowing that God has already given us a spirit of power, love, and discipline. [29]

The cause of many, if not most, of the ills of society today can be condensed into one three-word phrase. Be those ills dysfunctions in domestic relationships or outside relationships; in political, financial, or educational institutions; in children, youth, or adults; the same three-word phrase applies: *lack of discipline*. Social scientists, sociologists, psychologists, and political types of all stripes have offered many reasons for the negative trends affecting our society; nevertheless, undisciplined living is the major contributing factor.

In 2 Timothy 1:7, the Holy Spirit states, "For God has not given us a spirit of timidity, but of power, and love and discipline." The Greek noun from which our English word *discipline* is translated carries the basic meaning of one who has a sound mind, one who voluntarily places limitations on his freedoms and abilities as the result of proper thinking and thus demonstrates restraint in all his emotions, desires, and actions. More specifically, the word deals with the capability that produces self-control. Included in this concept are the concepts of instructing, teaching, and chastising. [30] So, the discipline to which this value refers is the discipline that is anchored in God; that is, divinely sourced discipline.

At its most basic level, discipline means structure, a concept contrary to the dominant theme in our culture. We live in a culture where the desire for instant gratification is the norm, where almost every behavior is discretionary, and where responsibility is generally placed somewhere other than with the individual. However, the structure required in divinely sourced discipline is a structure that conforms not to society's standard, but to God's.

Living that conforms to God's standard is living that conforms to God's original intent for the creation of humans and His purpose in giving life to each of us. That purpose is to undo the work of Satan and to bring us to share in His eternal holiness (Heb. 12:10). This type of structured living means our thinking, feeling, talking, and acting are organized daily according to the Word of God. It entails doing so in good times and bad, whether we want to or do not want to. Even if it brings pain and agony, we do it anyway, despite the discomfort. When our thinking, feeling, and acting are shaped by and brought under obedience to the Word of God, we will be perfected as God intended (2 Tim. 3:16–17).

In the incident recorded in Luke 5:1–11, Peter and his companions were faced with what can be described as one of those any-way-out or most-convenient-thing type situations.

Their response provides a clear example of how discipline produced by sound thinking works and how it can produce great results. These skilled and knowledgeable fishermen, who were thoroughly familiar with fishing on the Sea of Galilee, had fished all night without results and were on the shore washing their nets (vv. 2, 5) when they were instructed by a Galilean carpenter to "put out into the deep water and let your nets down for a catch" (v. 4). Their sound thinking, obviously shaped by some level of knowledge about Jesus, is shown in their reply to Jesus' invitation to resume fishing at a time they knew was not naturally conducive to catching fish. Clearly, they considered alternative action, as shown by Peter's response (v. 5).

But remember, divinely sourced discipline speaks to action controlled by sound thinking produced by a sound mind that has been trained by accurately processing information. Peter thus responded, "But at your bidding, I will let down the nets" (v. 5). What Peter and the others could not see because of their limited knowledge and ability, sound thinking assured them Jesus could see. What they did not know, sound thinking told them Jesus knew.

"And when they had done this . . ." (v. 6). Although these fishermen's natural instincts must have rebelled against what they were asked to do, sound thinking led them to action that controlled their natural instincts and caused them to obey the Lord's instruction. As a result of their disciplined action, they drew a quantity of fish beyond their expectation and imagination (vv. 6–7).

One reason some Christians do not experience fantastic results in their lives is that their minds have not been made sound by the Word of God. Their thinking is mixed with and gives almost equal validity to God's words, Dr. Phil's words, Oprah's words, the words of political correctness, and the words of their favorite authors. Consequently, their thinking is not disciplined by God's Word, and they do not do the necessary controlled actions. Peter and his companions had suffered a night of no success. But through sound thinking that led to controlled actions, they followed the directions of Jesus and enjoyed abundance beyond belief.

Imagine the stable, peaceful, tranquil, and productive life produced when a person exercises the divinely sourced discipline that is a product of faithful obedience to God's wisdom instead of human wisdom. In every account in Scripture where people were disciplined enough to obey the Lord—no matter how difficult the situation or how contrary to common wisdom—success was achieved. On the other hand, in every account where people did not obey the Lord—regardless of their reasons—failure was experienced.

Chapter 10

Change: God's Principles Versus Man's Theories (Part 5)

Divinely Sourced Values (Continued)

9. **Divinely sourced self-confidence:** This is the assurance we receive from patiently repeating a skill until we master it. It comes from using our gifts, talents, and abilities to show God's power, to proclaim His name, and to make known His glory. [31]

The *American Heritage Dictionary* provides four essential definitions of the noun *confidence:* "(1) trust or faith in a person or thing; (2) a trusting relationship; (3) a feeling of assurance, especially of self-assurance; and (4) the state or quality of being certain." [32]

Repetition is a key concept in this core value of divinely sourced self-confidence. However, the critical concept in this core value involves more than just repeatedly performing a skill, be it physical, mental, or emotional, until it is mastered. If that were the case, the attainment of this core value would simply be a matter of practice. Additionally, anyone may develop trust or faith in any person or thing and have a trusting relationship with any number of people. Feelings of assurance, especially of self-assurance, abound in all circles and are based on all kinds of evidence, and all kinds of things have led all kinds of people to a state or quality of being certain. The confidence of this value, therefore, must be anchored on a solid base with unchangeable conditions from an unshakable source.

The Bible plainly and forthrightly teaches the value of confidence. For example, Isaiah 30:15 says, "For thus says the Lord God, the Holy One of Israel: In returning and rest you shall be saved; in quietness and confidence shall be your strength." Hebrews 10:35 reads, "Therefore, do not throw away your confidence, which has a great reward." Furthermore, the Bible warns that confidence is not to be placed in possessions (Matt. 6:19–21; 1 Tim. 6:17) or in humans (Jer. 17:5). Self, all material possessions, and all humans will eventually fail. Confidence, therefore, must be placed in a source that is sure, stable, and everlasting, and there is but one who fits that bill—Jehovah God.

Scripture is full of encouraging admonitions regarding the source of true confidence. Proverbs 3:26 declares, "For the Lord will be your confidence, and will keep your foot from being caught"; and the same book later asserts, "In the fear of the Lord there is strong confidence, and His children will have refuge" (14:26). We are told by the Holy Spirit, "It is better to trust in the Lord than to have confidence in man" (Ps. 118:8).

As these verses clearly state, it is not enough just to have confidence, but the source of that confidence must be found in God rather than in humans. Human-sourced confidence—including self-confidence—stems from the sin-loving nature we inherited as the result of Adam and Eve's disobedience; it is a nature that is corrupt, deceitful, and evil (Eph. 4:22; Col. 3:9). But divinely sourced self-confidence derives from being God's new creation in Christ, a renewal according to the image of God and created in righteousness and truth (Eph. 4:22; Col. 3:10).

The Holy Spirit tells us, "Whatever you do in word and deed, do all in the name of the Lord Jesus Christ, giving thanks through Him to God the Father" (Col. 3:17). Therefore, the repetition of the right thing must be done for the right reason, which is to make God look good. In other words, in order for the repetition of skills, talents, or abilities to produce divinely sourced self-confidence, the action must have as its aim the goal of growing in righteousness and honoring God (1 Tim. 4:7; Heb. 5:14). Through repetition, a Christian develops the right kind of habits and trains his perceptions so that in any situation he is still able to reflect positively on the God he serves.

The *American Heritage Dictionary* lists another definition for confidence as "a tendency always to expect a favorable outcome." Was that not characteristic of Jesus? Did He not always expect a favorable outcome? When Jesus, along with His disciples, was on the way to Jerusalem, He said, "For He [the Son of man] will be delivered to the Gentiles, and will be mocked and mistreated and spit upon, and after they have scourged Him, they will kill Him; and the third day He will rise again" (Luke 18:32–33).

Confidence is also defined as "a condition in which one is free from doubt." Do we find that quality in the life of Jesus? We need look no further than His words when Peter drew his sword to protect Him (Matt. 26:52–53). When Jesus stood before Caiaphas on trial for His life, He confidently declared, "Hereafter you will see the Son of man sitting on the right hand of power, and coming on the clouds of heaven" (Matt. 26:64).

Confidence also carries the definition of "certainty in another's trustworthiness." Does this definition characterize the life of Jesus? Consider His words as He was breathing His last breath on the cross: "Father, into thy hands I commit [to deposit as a trust or for protection] My Spirit" (Luke 23:46).

We are seriously mistaken if we believe that confident Christian living comes easily and automatically. We are gravely wrong if we believe that proficiency in anything, whether physical, emotional, mental, or spiritual, comes through osmosis. Proficiency in Christian living—the ability to perform as needed, when needed, and at the level needed—comes through practice, through disciplined efforts repeated over and over again.

God's principle is stated thusly: "*Discipline* yourself for the purpose of godliness" (1 Tim. 4:7, emphasis added); and "Solid food is for the mature, who *because of practice* have their *senses trained* to discern good and evil" (Heb. 5:14, emphasis added). Undoubtedly, Jesus would have failed miserably that night in Gethsemane and succumbed to the terrible pressure were it not for this one fact: "He learned obedience from the things He suffered" (Heb. 5:8).

Jesus *learned* obedience, implying repeated practice. In His life, Jesus brought into existence the proficiency required to accept God's will, even at the cost of His own life. Through repeated practice, Jesus brought into existence the proficiency to say and mean, "Yet not My will, but Yours be done" (Luke 22:42). Through the value of divinely sourced self-confidence, Jesus lived a life that brought glory to God in all situations. Divinely sourced self-confidence will produce the same in the lives of all who, through repeated practice, live by it.

10. Divinely sourced self-worth: This value could be defined as the importance we place on our total well-being as a result of seeing ourselves as God sees us and not as the world sees us. Knowing that God indwells us through His Holy Spirit gives us the dignity of God-worth rather than other-worth, and this compels us to love and take care of our total being every day.[33]

Scholars almost uniformly acknowledge that possessing a sense of self-worth is a basic human need. However, at the same time, it is also a basic human problem. Why? The answer lies in the fact that so many people spend so much time and effort looking for self-worth. And just as people shape their desires and their actions by what they believe it will take to experience love, they essentially shape their desires and their actions by what they believe will increase their sense of self-worth.

But, like gold, there is real self-worth, and there is false self-worth. False self-worth may be as shiny and as sparkly as the real, but when it is assayed by time and circumstance, it proves its falsity. So many people spend so much time—some a lifetime—searching for self-worth, only to find an empty pot at the end of their rainbow of aspirations. In the parable of the prodigal son in Luke 15:11–21, for example, Jesus introduced His audience to a dissatisfied young man unable to differentiate between true and false self-worth and who did not know where true self-worth could be found. We will look at his story in more detail shortly.

Worth and *value* are synonymous terms and can be either innate or assigned; that is, either the object has the value it was created with or the object has a value assigned by another. As it pertains to humans, we recognize either the value God ascribes or the value the world ascribes. Throughout our lives, this world teaches us that the basis for evaluation (hence, the basis for self-worth) is determined by our skills, abilities, knowledge, material possessions, friends, colleagues, and the adulation we receive. Consequently, many people have fallen prey to others-worth, things-worth, and pride-worth. These are false foundations for evaluation.

We know this because the Bible says it in 1 John 2:15–17. Also, as far back as the prophet Jeremiah's time, God warned

His people about these false values (Jer. 9:23–24). The basis for true worth is contained in verse 24: " 'But let him who boasts boast of this, that he understands and knows Me, that I am the Lord who exercises lovingkindness, justice, and righteousness on earth; for I delight in these things,' declares the Lord." Furthermore, we should always keep in mind what Jesus taught about things esteemed by man: "For that which is highly esteemed among men is detestable in the sight of God" (Luke 16:15).

Our worth is established factually in two ways: (1) by being a product of God's creative activity and (2) by the price God was willing to pay to redeem us. But let us go back to our story of the prodigal son and look at this young man who, like so many today, did not understand this, but confused the false and the true and searched for worth in all the wrong places.

All change is birthed in dissatisfaction. Had the young man not been dissatisfied with who he was and where he was, he would not have clamored for change. Maybe he felt his self-assessed worth was underutilized. Perhaps he was not satisfied with his ability to fully use his intellectual prowess at home. He might have believed that better use could be made of the family's financial resources, or maybe he thought that with all he had going for him, he was being wasted at home. After all, who was there to notice or extol his self-perceived worth? Prompted by his dissatisfaction, he asked for his share of his father's wealth (v. 12).

The father gave him his inheritance, and the son "gathered everything together and went" (v. 13). His false sense of self-worth took him from his father and his brother, from his home and his friends, to journey to a distant country. He thought his dissatisfaction would become satisfaction once he escaped from his present circumstances. Unfortunately, this scene is repeated all too often today. People accepting false valuation and buying into self-worth as defined by society discard their true self-worth for society-defined worth. Like the prodigal, many of them end up in a distant country.

In that distant country, the young man encountered, virtually simultaneously, two unexpected surprises: (1) he ran out of money, and (2) a famine occurred. In very few words, Jesus describes how quickly and thoroughly the young man hit rock bottom: he was penniless, "and he began to be in need" (v. 14). The prodigal took a job that was both physically and religiously degrading—feeding pigs (pork was unclean to Jews). When a person does not value himself highly, he is subject to doing all kinds of degrading things. Because this young man's self-worth was others-worth, things-worth, and pride-worth, when others and things left his life, his pride quickly followed suit. Consequently, he ended up slopping hogs (v.15). The basis of the prodigal's self-worth led him to total humiliation; he ended up in a place where pigs were considered more valuable than he. Like the prodigal, many people, because of a wrong basis for self-worth, end up abusing their bodies instead of using them to fulfill the purpose for which God placed them on earth.

Jesus said, "But when he came to himself . . ." (v. 17). When a person seeks to live out a self-worth that is other than God's defined self-worth, that person is not truly himself. *Coming to himself* meant that the young man faced and accepted the truth of his condition. Living in shame and disgrace, he realized he had the potential for better things but was squandering his worth in a pigpen. He did not try to ignore, deny, or downplay the situation, as some might have done. He did not say, "I'm hungry, but I guess everybody else is too," or "I'm feeding pigs, but lots of others are doing the same thing." His decisions to enhance his self-worth had been stupid and had led him to a bad place. The truth he now accepted smashed his false pride and ego.

With a new perspective, the prodigal left the pigpen and determined to return, not just to his home, but to his father.

Neither excusing himself nor blaming others, he confessed his sin (vv. 18–19). Finally he could agree with what his father had known and told him all along: "This is not a good move, son. Moving away from home is not the best thing for you. All that you need is found here and in your relationships here at home."

Upon his return, the young man received no recrimination from his father, only pure love, forgiveness, and acceptance. The father saw the worth that his son could not see. Notice, it was at home that the prodigal found the worth he had sought in vain in a distant country. And the worth the father saw was not in his son's healthy body, good looks, or financial resources; his worth lay solely in the fact that he was his son.

We are creatures created in God's image. God gave us gifts, talents, and abilities; God gave us our self-worth. The things valued by society change with time, location, and custom, but God's standard of worth remains constant through time, varying conditions, and diverse cultures. Divinely sourced self-worth is based on our innate worth as bestowed by God. As we recognize and accept God's standard of worth, reject others-worth, things-worth, and pride-worth, and as we move toward fulfilling God's purpose for our lives, we are, in fact, living out the core value of divinely sourced self-worth.

11. Divinely sourced self-respect: This value could be described as the approval God gives or withholds from us based on our obedience to Him and submission to His Word in our thoughts, words, and actions. It is recognizing that human respect is given or withheld based on merit and how we assume responsibility for our own thoughts, words, and actions. [34]

The phrase *self-respect* means "due respect for oneself, one's character, and one's conduct." [35] In other words, it is appreciating one's self as having worth and importance. Within the definition of self-respect are several critical concepts to understanding true, divinely sourced self-respect and its biblical foundation; these include *self*, *respect*, *due*, *character*, and *conduct*.

Divinely sourced self-respect is based on true information, and true information is information anchored in God's Word. All truth is God's truth; any "truth" in conflict with God's truth is not truth. True information is realized in relationship with Jesus Christ (John 14:6; 8:31–32). Only then are we able to understand the value, the worth, and the esteem God gives. It is that experiential understanding that forms the bedrock foundation for divinely sourced self-respect.

The "self" in *self-respect* refers to the total, essential, or particular being of a person; it is, in essence, the individual. Thus in self-respect, the focus is not on the recognition held by others, but rather on the recognition the individual has of himself. It is true that the Bible condemns self-focus or self-centeredness, because that would be selfishness. However, one must have a measure of awareness of self in order to comply with God's commands involving self-exaltation (Matt. 23:12), self-control (2 Pet. 1:5), self-denial (Matt. 16:24), and appropriate love of others (Matt. 22:39).

"Respect" in *self-respect* simply involves the showing of consideration or appreciation. As Christians, we are God's workmanship (Eph. 2:10). God is working in us (Phil. 2:12–13), and we are temples of the Holy Spirit (1 Cor. 6:19–20). Can we truly be pleasing to God if we fail to be appreciative of what He has made us, what He is doing in us, and where He chooses to dwell?

The definition of self-respect also speaks of "due respect," which is something that is justly deserved. It speaks to the actions of sowing and reaping, something deserved as a result of something done. The law of sowing and reaping (Gal. 6:7–8) applies not just to eternal things, but to temporal things as well. It affects what we do here on earth and what we receive while here on earth. In terms of due respect for one's character and conduct, we must be careful not to confuse character with reputation. Reputation is what others think of us, but character is what we are: our essential and distinctive elements. What we are, not what we have or what others think of us, is what expresses our essential worth.

Self-respect is birthed in the value we place on what others think of us. In turn, that determines the respect we receive from others; that is, how others perceive us and are impacted by our lives, thoughts, and actions. In other words, people accord to us respect based on their assessment of us. However, people award respect based on all kinds of things, and people respect in themselves all kinds of acts and qualities, all of which may be moral or immoral, good or bad, positive or negative, constructive or destructive. Consequently, it is necessary to clearly distinguish divinely sourced self-respect from all other types of self-respect. The foundation on which divinely sourced self-respect rests is the intrinsic worth, value, and esteem God imbued in each person. Therefore, to maintain its identity and its health, divinely sourced self-respect dictates that one think, feel, and behave in keeping with his divine worth, value, and esteem. In other words, he must think, feel, and act toward himself and others as God does.

What then is the conduct on which due respect should be based? Our conduct is the channel through which the condition and thoughts of our heart are made known to others (Prov. 4:23; 23:7). Our conduct is the demonstration of the life lived in the mind, the unspoken sermon we preach every day. What type of conduct creates the right respect? The conduct that brings God's approval, thus the self-respect of this value, is measured by the degree to which one's life and work beautify the character and ministry of our Lord Jesus Christ (Phil. 2:14–16; Rom. 14:17–18).

Therefore, the most important element in divinely sourced self-respect is a function of one's relationship with God. Interwoven throughout His entire life and teachings is Jesus' assertion that a person's relationship with God is the most important relationship in life. From a healthy relationship with God, we gain a sense of true worth, value, and esteem. This, in turn, produces a correct view of life and all its various elements, including the foundation on which the valuing of the respect given by others, as well as the respect one accords himself, is based. Keeping that single relationship with God as the most important relationship in one's life is no complicated matter. It is simply a matter of commitment of heart, soul, and mind (Matt. 22:37–39).

12. Divinely sourced intimacy: This type of intimacy is characterized by the love we show in our single most important relationship with God, which is the main thing in our lives. This love for God, in turn, affects the love we have in every other significant relationship. As we love God, so do we love ourselves; and as we love ourselves, so do we love everyone else in our lives. This is how we keep the main thing, the main thing.[36]

There exists in each of us the God-given need for connectivity with other humans; that is, close, intimate relationships with other people. We are not designed to be little islands of our own, separated from and independent of everyone else. By the very nature of things, it is impossible to live an isolated life; the Bible teaches, "For none of us lives to himself, and none of us dies to himself" (Rom. 14:7). Unfortunately, in our sex-crazed society, the word *intimacy* has almost completely assumed connotations of something sexual. One of the unfortunate by-products of this mislabeling is that real intimacy is rare while sex is all too common.

Genuine intimacy is a shared sense of openness. It is the ability to be who and what we are with another person, who is able to do the same with us. The more we are able to be ourselves in a relationship, the more intimate the relationship becomes; and in some relationships, intimacy does properly include sex. However, intimacy is much more than sex. Intimacy includes all aspects of our lives with others: the physical, social, emotional, mental, and spiritual. It includes important nonsexual aspects as well, such as love, respect, emotional openness, commitment, kindness, and communication. True intimacy is the perfect fulfilling of the human need for deep, meaningful connectivity with others; it is the most profound connection between two souls, independent of sexual contact.

We humans are a needy people; even the richest, strongest, prettiest, most skilled, and most noted among us is needy. Although many refuse to recognize it, one of our strongest needs—if not the strongest—is the need for intimacy with God. We all need God at the core of our lives. God created humans with a fundamental yearning for permanent, intimate, and productive fellowship with Him. There is a hole, as it were, built into each of us that can be filled only by God Himself. Although many do not recognize or accept this yearning, it is there, nonetheless. Augustine said it well: "Thou [God] hast created us for Thyself, and our heart is not quiet till it rests in Thee."[37]

Having an intimate, joyful, peaceful relationship with almighty God is the most important foundation for all other relationships in life. That intimate relationship with God gives strength and focus to our marriage, working relationships, and friendships—in short, all other human relationships. So, divinely sourced intimacy is a deep emotional connection first with God and then with self and others; however, it is the connection with God that provides the deepest source of mental, emotional, psychological, and spiritual strength.

When God created humans, He created them with His nature stamped upon them. Created in His image, they strive to fulfill that yearning for permanency, intimacy, and productivity. However, since Adam and Eve's sin in the garden, God's creatures have failed to live up to His image. Instead of fulfilling their inborn yearning for Him, they seek to fulfill it in relationships with others or with what one writer termed "popular anesthetics": wealth, fame, achievements, entertainment, illicit relationships, alcohol, cocaine, or other types of nerve deadeners. Some of those popular anesthetics work, but only for a short period of time, soon losing their effectiveness. That's because nothing but God can fill the void.

Divinely sourced intimacy says that true satisfaction in life is never attained until we come to know the living God personally and intimately (Matt. 4:1–10; Mark 12:28–32). We must be intimate with God before we can be intimate with ourselves, and we must be intimate with ourselves before we can be intimate with others. As one writer said it, "*I* need to be present before *we* can evolve. In other words, true intimacy in our relationships with others is an outgrowth of the true intimacy we experience first in our relationship with God.

For us to experience this kind of love in our relationships with others, we must first experience God's love for us. The Holy Spirit states, "We love, because He first loved us" (1 John 4:19). So the only way we can consistently demonstrate this type of love toward others is to experience being loved this way by God. Only by starting with God can we understand what love is, what love means, and what love does.

The Holy Spirit tells us that "love is from God" and that "God is love" (1 John 4:7–8); in other words, our duty for this type of love grows out of the nature of the love we share with God Himself. Love not only expresses God's nature but also has its source in God. By imitating the way in which God loves us, we discover the way to receiving and giving love to others, thus creating intimate relationships anchored in who God is and what God does.

Chapter 11

Change: God's Principles Versus Man's Theories (Part 6)

Divinely Sourced Values (Continued)

Divinely Sourced Change

Once one identifies those values that are meaningful in terms of effectively living out a relationship with God, development of strategies to implement those values is required. For many Christians, implementing Jesus' core values requires changing from something that has become comfortable to something that appears somewhat uncomfortable. It means perhaps doing something one has never done before or doing something one is not used to doing, and that is living by values, the extent of which is totally foreign to the wisdom of this world.

However, even here the Holy Spirit supplies what is needed by providing an overall strategy that subsequently produces all other successful strategies. The Holy Spirit not only identifies the one who is to serve as the target and model of the values we should form, but He also provides a very clear and concise plan to implement those values. But because of the humanistic thinking that has so invaded the church of our Lord, many Christians have fallen prey to the false belief that something as difficult as changing one's basic makeup can be accomplished only with the help of specially trained professionals using the latest in modern information and techniques. Additionally, although many Christians will see the necessity of reforming their values to mirror divinely sourced values and will even strive diligently to do so, the degree of success will not be equal to the numbers making the attempt or the efforts expended. However, when such desires and efforts are divinely sourced, when they come from God and are based on God's Word, God's wisdom, and God nature, success is assured, no matter the severity of the change needed. A key passage that shows the elements of this assured change is Ephesians 4:17–24:

1. Putting off the old: A key starting point for change is the recognition that living by values other than values sourced in God amounts to living on the level of those who have not been regenerated. For this reason, the Holy Spirit, through the apostle Paul, writes, "This I say therefore, and affirm together with the Lord, that you walk [live] no longer just as the Gentiles also walk, in the futility of their mind. . . . Lay aside [put off] the old self which is being corrupted in accordance with the lusts of deceit" (Eph. 4:17, 22). That which must be put off is the old self, that by which all too many Christians seek to live functional, abundant lives and the source of values when those values are not divinely sourced. It is the product of deceit, born out of a lie Satan sold to our first parents. It was corrupted when Adam and Eve fell, and it is constantly being corrupted today. It is disobedient and rebellious, futile in its thinking and darkened in it understanding, following a pattern of disobedience (vv. 17–19).

In contrast, the Holy Spirit says that Christians "have not learned Christ in this way [to live by the standards of unsaved people is incompatible with the teachings of Christ], if indeed you have heard Him and have been taught in Him, just as truth is in Jesus, that in reference to your former manner of life [the life you lived before being saved], you lay aside the old self which is being corrupted in accordance with the lusts of deceit, and that you be renewed in the spirit of your mind" (Eph. 4:20–23).

2. Renewal of the mind: Divinely sourced change involves renewal; that is, making new again in the spirit of the mind. According to Titus 3:5, one ministry of the Holy Spirit is to restore what was ruined as a result of the fall of Adam and Eve: "He [God] saved us . . . by the washing of regeneration and renewing [making new] by the Holy Spirit." This is "the renewing of the mind" (Rom. 12:2) to a "true knowledge, according to the One who created him [the new self]" (Col. 3:10).

The *mind* refers not only to our abilities of perception through our various senses and our understanding, but it also references our abilities of feeling, judging, and determining. According to the *Lexicon to the Old and New Testaments* edited by Spiros Zodhiates, the mind is the organ of the consciousness preceding action or recognizing and judging action.[38] Through the ministry of the Holy Spirit, the Christian is enabled to begin the process of renouncing the old pattern of life with the old worldly based values and accepting the new pattern of life with the new divinely sourced values. He begins the process of exchanging the old way of thinking, feeling, and judging with the new way of thinking, feeling, and judging. How is this done? The answer is found through a very simple yet profound process.

In the words of the Holy Spirit, it involves the taking of "every thought [that is, the mind, thoughts, purpose] captive to the obedience of Christ" (2 Cor. 10:5). All of our thinking has to be brought under the authority of Christ. Why is the mind so critical in the process? It is simple, really. The mind is where action begins. "Watch over your heart with all diligence, for from it flow the springs of life," says Proverbs 4:23.

Every action is determined by what a person thinks and believes. As Burton Coffman in his commentary on Proverbs states, "The heart, as the word is used in the Bible, means the mind, which is the center of human intelligence, emotions and the will. The fact here stated is that the whole moral conduct of human life, and its every action, attitude, and purpose are determined by what one thinks and believes." [39] To change behavior, then, the thoughts that produce the behavior must be changed. To act like Jesus, our thoughts must be changed to be like His thoughts; hence, the exhortation of Philippians 2:5 (see also Prov. 23:7; Matt. 15:18–20; Luke 6:45).

3. Obedience, not feelings: Another key factor in the accomplishment of change requires Christians to live, not by feelings, but by God's commandments, or "commandments-based living," as Jay Adams terms it in *Godliness Through Discipline*.[40] It is the understanding that such change is a divine imperative and is to be obeyed regardless of feelings. It is the understanding that one must obey God, not because such obedience constitutes actions one necessarily feels like taking, but because God mandates such action. In many cases, the feelings follow the actions.

4. Disciplined living: In 1 Timothy 4:7, God's instruction is to "discipline yourself for the purpose of godliness." In other words, we must structure, set up, and organize ourselves for the purpose of being like God. This requires a life oriented, set up, organized, and running day by day toward the goal of feeling, thinking, talking, and behaving like Jesus.[41] Consequently, reforming one's values into the values of Jesus is not a quick, overnight, minimal-effort undertaking. It takes the determination to be like Jesus, it takes time, and it takes consistent and concerted effort. Those three things are achieved only through consistently practicing obedience to God's Word.

5. Denial of self: In this context of daily, sustained efforts toward becoming more like Jesus, we can better understand the import of Jesus' words in Luke 9:23: "If anyone wishes to come after Me, let him deny himself, and take up his cross daily, and follow Me." As stated previously, living by Jesus' values takes us beyond familiar, comfortable territory into the unknown and uncomfortable. Living in a society in which the phrase "self-preservation is the first law of nature" is commonly quoted, we tend to rebel at any requirement that places self in position other than first.

This area of self-denial is a major area of false beliefs and reasoning among many Christians. But Jesus is not talking about denying self of something for some misplaced reason. For example, a Christian may be disturbed by his wrong action and feel quite guilty. In an attempt to make things right, to assuage his guilty conscience, he may decide to deny himself something, such as the buying of a new device he has had his eyes on for the past month. This, however, is not what biblical self-denial is all about; the biblical concept of self-denial is to deny self itself. It is to deny old desires, ways, practices, and patterns (see Rom. 6:11; Gal. 6:14). In other words, self must be denied, and the cross must be taken up daily.

There is another area of misconception on the part of many Christians. When they suffer rejection or have a difficult time with their spouses, children, or employers, they mistakenly conclude, "Well, that's just my cross." Such is not the meaning of Jesus' words here in Luke 9:23. This taking up the cross involves a day-by-day battle within, a putting to death the old pattern of living. It means saying yes and no: yes to Jesus and no to self. It involves a decision to follow Jesus and His pattern of living each day and doing it until it becomes second nature. Here again, such action takes time. However, if we stick with it long enough and behave like Jesus long enough, practicing what God tells us to do by following in the steps of Jesus, the values by which Jesus lived will become our values.

6. The power of the Holy Spirit: Another key in incorporating the core values of Jesus is the recognition that no Christian is able to incorporate these values on his own. The good news, however, is we are not alone. We have the unconquerable and inexhaustible power of God through the indwelling of His Spirit. To prevent the discouragement that often overtakes us when we try to accomplish something difficult and beyond our strength, we must remember that we are not left alone in our own strength to conform to the pattern of Jesus' life. God is there, ever working to bring about our conformity to His pattern, and the power of the Holy Spirit is an ever-present force (Phil. 2:13; 1 John 4:4; Phil. 4:13). We have the power of God's indwelling Spirit to help us as we strive to substitute our values with Jesus' values.

The power of the Holy Spirit in the life of the Christian is yet another area fraught with misunderstanding. Some Christians have made the work of the Holy Spirit mystical, "twistical," and incomprehensible. They say it is a work that cannot be understood; it is something that just happens. Still other Christians believe that the work of the Holy Spirit is totally independent of any effort on the part of the Christian; the Holy Spirit does it all, they say.

Although this manuscript is not a treatise on the work of the Holy Spirit, suffice it to say, the Holy Spirit does not act absent from or contrary to the Bible, the Word of God. The Bible is the Holy Spirit's book; the Holy Spirit Himself inspired it and authored it. He guided approximately forty men over a period of fifteen hundred years to produce this book. God, through His providence, has preserved this book century after century after century, despite the efforts of atheists, agnostics, skeptics, critics, and others who have tried to destroy it or render it useless. After all God did to produce and to preserve this book, and after all the sacrifices of those people God used in producing and preserving this book, the idea that the Holy Spirit zaps an instant state of discipline apart from His book lacks any sign of logical reasoning. The Holy Spirit works through His Word. The Bible is the powerful and effective tool through which He accomplishes His work (Eph. 6:17; Heb. 4:12).

7. Perfecting through the Scriptures: In 2 Timothy 3:15–17, the Bible speaks of four things the Word of God does for those who commit to obeying it. This passage refers to "the sacred writings which are able to give you the wisdom that lead to salvation through faith which is in Christ Jesus" and states that "all Scripture is inspired by God and profitable for teaching, for reproof, for correction, for training in righteousness; that the man of God may be adequate, equipped for every good work." In other words, the Bible (1) teaches us what God requires, (2) convicts us of sin by showing us when we fall short of God's requirements, (3) sets us straight again, and (4) trains us in what God defines as right. In short, Scripture trains and disciplines the Christian who commits to obeying it. It provides structured training in how to think, feel, talk, and act like Jesus, and it helps us to avoid those things contrary to His thinking, feeling, talking, and acting.

The Bible teaches that in Christ God frees us from all the things that bind us to our lower nature; that is, our old wants, needs, and desires. But this freedom comes only through the structure found in God's Word (Rom. 8:1–2; Gal. 5:1) and obedience to it. There is no such thing as ad-libbing the incorporation of Jesus' values. There is no such thing as serendipitously acquiring them. There is no such thing as just waking up one morning and suddenly living by the values of Jesus. Exchanging earth-based values for heaven-based values occurs only through structured discipline attained through obedience to God's Word. There is no other way.

So then, to be structurally trained in adopting and living out divinely sourced values, one must do what God says to do and refrain from doing what God says not to do. Such success is achieved in four specific ways: (1) as the study of God's Word becomes a regular part of one's daily routine, (2) as prayerful obedience becomes a priority, (3) as one does what the Bible says and according to its schedule, and (4) as one obeys what it says regardless of feelings.

Conclusion

To the critics who claim that the existence of so many Christians who live dysfunctional, unfulfilled lives is clear evidence that the Bible is not capable of effectively addressing the many complex problems people encounter in today's complex age, and to those critics who deny the effectiveness of the Bible based on the fact that all too many Christians fail to display the character of the Lord they claim to follow, the answer is the same. To modify the famous saying of G. K. Chesterton, the principles of living contained in the Bible have not been tried and found wanting. They are, however, difficult and have thus been left untried.

To all Christians struggling with dysfunctional, unfulfilled living, the question Jesus posed to the lame man in John 5:1–9 is the one they, too, must answer: "Do you wish to get well?" (v. 6). Do you so long to become well that you will do whatever needs to be done in order to get well? God has made all necessary provisions for you to live a functional, fulfilled, abundant life. However, it is up to you to provide the desire that is strong enough to do what God says to do. Living any quality of life less than the abundant life Jesus died to give represents unrealized opportunities.

Reflections

How has the material in this study guide changed your thinking? _____
_____
_____
_____
_____
_____
_____
_____

How will you apply the material you have learned? _____
_____
_____
_____
_____
_____
_____
_____

Questions for Study

Chapter 1: Unrealized Opportunities

1. In recent centuries, in what grand deception has Satan succeeded in convincing many people, including Christians, to believe? _____
_____

2. True ___ or False ___: All Christians experience the gift of abundant living (John 10:9–10).

3. Describe the 10/90 rule. _____
_____

4. How does the 10/90 rule affect the true quality of one's life? _____
_____

Chapter 2: The True Information from the True Source

1. Effective information is necessary to functional living. How does the author define "effective information"? _____
_____
_____

2. What are the only two sources of information, or the only two voices of authority?

    a. _____

    b. _____

3. What are two factors that make God's Word indispensable to humans' ability to experience true fulfillment?

    a. _____

    b. _____

Authenticity

1. Why is it important for Christians to believe the Bible we have today reflects the actual words God originally inspired? _____
_____
_____

2. True ___ or False ___ : The accuracy of the Old Testament we have today is supported by the following facts: (a) it agrees with the Septuagint, the Greek translation of the Old Testament, which dates from the third century BC; (b) there is substantial agreement between all the ancient manuscripts of the Old Testament in existence today; and (3) the Dead Sea Scrolls were written about a thousand years before any of the Old Testament manuscripts we have.

3. True ___ or False ___ : There are many more manuscripts and copies of portions of Homer's *Iliad* and Caesar's *Gallic Wars* than there are New Testament documents.

4. What is the earliest date of some of the copies of New Testament documents we have today? _____

Bible Translations

1. Why must Christians take care in selecting a Bible translation? _____
_____
_____

2. Give a brief description of the five categories of English translations.

    a. _____
    b. _____
    c. _____
    d. _____
    e. _____

Dangerous Focus

1. Translations designed to be more contemporary in expression and more acceptable to the masses face a joint danger. What is it? _____
_____
_____

2. True ___ or False ___: Only the major ideas of the Bible are important; therefore, changing words is really not a big deal.

3. True ___ or False ___: God's thoughts and ways are very compatible to human's thoughts and ways, and humans can easily understand the depth of meaning of the words God breathed out; therefore, accurately choosing words to substitute for God's words is a relatively simple matter.

Chapter 3: The All-Sufficiency of the Bible (Part 1)

Prevalent Beliefs

1. Briefly describe the following claims made by critics regarding the ability of the Bible to address human problems today.

    a. Inappropriate use: _____
_____

    b. Combining: _____
_____

    c. There all the time: _____
_____

    d. Ineffective results:_____
_____

Reshaping the Faith

Humanism:
1. True ___ or False ___: Humanism is a doctrine, attitude, or way of life centered on interests and values as seen by God.

2. True ___ or False ___: Humanism is the doctrine that human dignity, worth, and capacity for self-realization occur through acceptance of God's Word.

3. True ___ or False ___: Humanism teaches that the enhancing of human freedom and dignity is dependent on the individual experiencing limited civil liberties.

Political Correctness:
1. True ___ or False ___: As taught today, the aim of political correctness is to eliminate words and actions designed to offend and to unlawfully exclude people.

2. True ___ or False ___: Political correctness contains the idea that some ideas should be rejected because there are some ideas, including religion, that are better than other ideas.

3. True ___ or False ___: As a result of the influence of political correctness, the teaching and the preaching of biblical doctrines is less threatened.

4. True ___ or False ___: The Bible teaches that the church's responsibility is to avoid offense in living and teaching biblical truth.

Subjectivism:
1. True ___ or False ___: Subjectivism is the belief that there are no objective principles of conduct that apply to all people in all situations.

2. True ___ or False ___: Subjectivism contains the idea that the individual's own perceptions, opinions, experiences, inclinations, and desires determine the rightness or the wrongness of his behavior.

Relativism:
1. True ___ or False ___: Ethical relativism is the belief that God has established moral and ethical standards applicable to all people in all ages and cultures.

2. True ___ or False ___: Situational relativism is the belief that concepts of "good" and "bad" are established by the cultures in which the actions occur.

3. True ___ or False ___: Cognitive relativism is the belief in an objective standard of truth and a universal giver of truth.

***Pluralism*:**

1. True ___ or False ___: The main idea contained in pluralism is that of diversity and tolerance.

2. True ___ or False ___: In pluralism, all religious belief systems and philosophies are of equal validity.

3. True ___ or False ___: To conform to the idea of pluralism, all religions must be constructed so that their actions and doctrines are not offensive to the followers of any other religion.

Chapter 4: The All-Sufficiency of the Bible (Part 2)

The Bible Unmixed

1. What definition does the author give for the term *syncretism*? _____
_____
_____

2. What two factors give momentum to the desire of many Christians to accommodate to the majority culture?

    a. _____
    b. _____

3. True ___ or False ___: The teaching of John 17:17 is that God's Word is the final standard of what is true and what is not true.

4. What standard do Scriptures such as Jeremiah 23:28; Deuteronomy 4:2 and 12:32; Proverbs 30:6; and Matthew

15:3 establish regarding the mixing of human words with God's Word? _____
_____
_____

5. True ___ or False ___: Changing the world for Christ can be more effectively accomplished when the message is more acceptable to society.

The Peril of Christian Counseling

1. True ___ or False ___: The field of Christian counseling presents a safe and effective option for Christians who desire to honor God in their lives.

2. True ___ or False ___: The basic foundation of the present-day Christian counseling industry is the desire to honor God as Creator and His Word as His guide for daily living.

3. True ___ or False ___: The field of Christian counseling has little or no identity with the theories advanced by Charles Darwin (theory of evolution) and Sigmund Freud (the father of psychoanalysis).

4. From the following list, select some areas in which the theory of evolution and postmodern thinking have shaped the practice of Christian counseling.

    ___ a. Control and guidance of the individual reside with a power beyond the individual.
    ___ b. God's Word is deemed not applicable to the problems of human life.
    ___ c. Mankind was created by God and is accountable to Him.

___ d. The source of knowledge resides outside of individual experience.
___ e. Ultimately, humans are able to overcome the impact of how they have been shaped by their environment.
___ f. Because of the influence of their environment, humans are unable to make free choices.
___ g. The need of the individual is always paramount to the needs of the whole.
___ h. All values, rights, and duties originate from a power beyond the individual.
___ i. There is no universal standard of right and wrong.
___ j. True functional living can be achieved only in relationship with God.

Chapter 5: The All-Sufficiency of the Bible (Part 3)

The Perfect Work of the Holy Spirit

1. True ___ or False ___: If care is taken when selecting them, theories of man can be included to improve the effectiveness of God's Word in addressing human problems.

2. True ___ or False ___: The Bible ceases to be the ultimate standard of functional living when large numbers of Christians are unable to experience functional living.

3. When a Christian mixes human theories with the Word of God, he is demonstrating a lack of _____ in the effectiveness of God's Word to accomplish God's purpose and is proclaiming that the Bible is not the standard of ultimate truth.

Functional Living God's Way

4. True ___ or False ___: Generally, when human theories are added to the Word of God, such theories are changed to conform to biblical principles.

5. Because of the _____ nature of the Word of God, true functional living is _____ on nothing else.

Chapter 6: Change: God's Principles Versus Man's Theories (Part 1)

The Approach Is Critical

1. True ___ or False ___: What humans believe about human nature shapes their view of both behavior and needed changes; and the most complete and effective source of knowledge about human nature is the scientific study of the origin of humans, their behavior, and their social and cultural development.

2. True ___ or False ___: The views of man prevalent in human theories can properly identify the needed change and produce biblical principles that in turn produce biblical techniques of change.

3. Which of the following two paints a picture of humans as basically good: human theories or God's Word? (Underline the correct answer.)

4. The Bible teaches that the factors affecting and shaping human behavior are of what type: external or internal? (Underline the correct answer.)

5. True ___ or False ___: Human theories teach that humans are insufficient within themselves to live up to their full potential.

6. Select the factors that are necessary to true functional living:

    ___ a. Knowledge of God
    ___ b. Yielding to the Holy Spirit
    ___ c. Involvement in the work of the church
    ___ d. A and B
    ___ e. All of the above

7. No matter how _____ or how _____ to human wisdom, the instructions given in the Bible will produce the exact results God intends.

Functional Living

1. To achieve functional living, it is necessary to understand that actions do not just materialize out of thin air; rather, a person's actions are always functions of the _____ that person holds.

2. True ___ or False ___: When a Christian experiences dysfunctional living, it is usually the result of living by worldly values.

3. To experience functional living requires _____ that will result in making _____ combination of choices that produce functional living.

4. Our personal values are the _____ we place on what we _____ is most important in our lives.

5. Which of the following compose our personal values?

   ___ a. The rules we live by, which in turn determine what we do each day.
   ___ b. Our view of the world around us, which in turn determines how we display our beliefs.
   ___ A but not B
   ___ B but not A
   ___ Neither A nor B
   ___ Both A and B

6. True ___ or False ___: Our personal values have little or no impact on the lives we live on a daily basis.

7. The standard that must be used in formulating or reforming the values necessary to functional living is God's standard, man's standard, or both. (Underline the correct answer.)

8. True ___ or False ___: The values by which one lives are relatively unimportant as long as those values result in the person being a good citizen.

9. True ___ or False ___: There are only two sources of values: God's wisdom and human wisdom.

10. True ___ or False ___: When a Christian experiences inconsistent Christian living, it is usually because there is a lack of harmony in the personal values held by that Christian.

11. The world's system teaches that the basis of personal values consists of _____ prowess, physical _____, material _____, _____ achievements, and the approval of _____.

12. According to Jeremiah 9:23–24, the things God delights in are a person who _____ and _____ Him, who knows that He is the Lord who exercises lovingkindness, _____, and righteousness on earth.

Chapter 7: Change: God's Principles Versus Man's Theories (Part 2)

Jesus Is the Answer

1. Values are gained and reformed largely through mimicking significant, credible, authoritative people. Which significant, credible, authoritative person should Christians mimic? ___

2. True ___ or False ___: The only way the false values of the world can be countered is through internalizing the values by which Jesus lived.

3. True ___ or False ___: A Christian can achieve value clarification only as he determines his truths, beliefs, and ideas and how they motivate him.

4. In Matthew 22:37–38, Jesus taught and demonstrated that one's _____ with God has to be the most _____ relationship in his life.

5. True ___ or False ___: The Holy Spirit uses a Christian's obedience to form in him the values consistent with the quality of life Christians are called to live.

Chapter 8: Change: God's Principles Versus Man's Theories (Part 3)

Divinely Sourced Values

1. Jesus' life and teachings cover the entire array of human _____, _____, and _____.

2. True ___ or False ___: Divinely sourced values are values based on God's principles and are empowered by His Holy Spirit.

Divinely Sourced Honesty:
1. True ___ or False ___: Divinely sourced honesty deals with integrity in one's relationships, beginning with honesty in one's relationship with God.

2. In His trial in the wilderness as recorded in Matthew 4, Jesus demonstrated divinely sourced honesty in His relationship with God by relying on and being faithful to God's _____.

Divinely Sourced Courage:
1. True ___ or False ___: Divinely sourced courage is living by God's standard of right and wrong regardless of the personal cost to the individual.

2. List three events where Jesus demonstrated divinely sourced courage.
    a. _____
    b. _____
    c. _____

Divinely Sourced Forgiveness:

1. Divinely sourced forgiveness relates to the ability to _____ and _____ God's concept of forgiveness to work in all of one's relationships.

2. Luke 23:43 does/does not demonstrate what it means to live by the value of divinely sourced forgiveness? (Underline the correct answer).

3. What are the three conditions for which divinely sourced forgiveness is mandated?
    a. _____
    b. _____
    c. _____

Divinely Sourced Power:

1. True ___ or False ___: Divinely sourced power deals with the ability to choose how one responds to any situation in life.

2. True ___ or False ___: Having the right information is critical to the process of determining how to respond to any situation.

3. In guiding us in the choices we make, God gives us His inspired _____ and the power of His _____.

Chapter 9: Change: God's Principles Versus Man's Theories (Part 4)

<u>Divinely Sourced Values (Continued)</u>

Divinely Sourced Purpose:
1. Divinely sourced purpose means that one is seeking to live out the _____ for which God created _____.

2. True ___ or False ___: Living by the value of divinely sourced purpose enables one to experience the good that God can bring out of any situation.

3. How does the parable of the fig tree in Luke 13:6–9 demonstrate the concept of divinely sourced purpose? ____
_____
_____

Divinely Sourced Excellence:
1. True ___ or False ___: Divinely sourced excellence speaks to faith in God and its impact on how one faces the circumstances of life.

2. True ___ or False ___: Divinely sourced excellence is developed and strengthened as one trusts God and shows that trust in everyday living.

Divinely Sourced Self-Image:
1. True ___ or False ___: Our self-image is a function of how we describe ourselves in relationship to others.

2. True ___ or False ___: Divinely sourced self-image results as one accepts the fact of being God's masterpiece and realizes the provision God has made for living the abundant life both here and in heaven.

Divinely Sourced Discipline:
1. Divinely sourced discipline speaks to the ability to _____ what God says, _____ it when it should done, even if pain or isolation is involved.

2. In Luke 5:1–11, how do Peter and his companions demonstrate the divinely sourced discipline that comes from a mind trained by Jesus' teachings? _____
_____
_____

Chapter 10: Change: God's Principles Versus Man's Theories (Part 5)

Divinely Sourced Values (Continued)

Divinely Sourced Self-Confidence:
1. True ___ or False ___: Divinely sourced self-confidence is developed as Christians practice the right kinds of habits, training their perceptions so that in any situation they will still be able to live a truly functional life.

2. The objective to be achieved through living by the value of divinely sourced self-confidence is to bring into one's life the proficiency to consistently show God's _____, to proclaim God's _____, and to make known God's _____.

Divinely Sourced Self-Worth:
1. True ___ or False ___: A Christian is living by the value of divinely sourced self-worth when he sees himself as God sees him, and, from that view, gives special effort to care for his total being (spirit, soul, and body).

Functional Living God's Way

2. Being a product of God's creative activity and understanding the price that God was willing to pay to redeem us are factors that do/do not factually establish our worth? (Underline the correct answer.)

3. In the parable of the prodigal son (Luke 15:11–21), what actions taken by the young son revealed that he and his father did not share the same view of the son's worth to the family? _____
_____
_____

Divinely Sourced Self-Respect:
1. True ___ or False ___: A key element in divinely sourced self-respect is that of taking responsibility for thoughts, words, and actions and consistently placing them under the authority of God's Word.

2. Divinely sourced self-respect is based on _____ information that is realized in one's _____ with Jesus Christ.

3. True ___ or False ___: The conduct upon which divinely sourced self-respect is based is conduct that is accepted and approved by fellow humans.

Divinely Sourced Intimacy:
1. True ___ or False ___: True intimacy can occur only in a sexual relationship between two people.

2. True ___ or False ___: For divinely sourced intimacy to occur, one's love relationship with God has to be the single most important relationship in life.

3. True ___ or False ___: True intimacy can be experienced in a person's relationships only as he experiences true intimacy in his relationship with God.

4. True ___ or False ___: Being divine made it easy for Jesus to live by divinely sourced values.

5. Jesus' life was perfect because He _____ _____ obedience through the things in life He _____.

Chapter 11: Change: God's Principles Versus Man's Theories (Part 6)

Divinely Sourced Values (Continued)

Divinely Sourced Change:
1. True ___ or False ___: Success in changing one's values can be accomplished only with the assistance of a specially trained professional.

2. True ___ False ___: Divinely sourced change is change that comes from God and is based on God's Word, God's wisdom, and God's nature.

3. Ephesians 4:17–24 teaches that God's method of change involves a _____ off the _____ self, and a renewal in the _____ of the _____.

4. True ___ or False ___: Every Christian has been equipped by God to comply with God's method of change.

5. Describe the difference between feelings-based living and commandments-based living. _____
_____
_____

6. True ___ or False ___: Changing one's values to divinely sourced values is a process that can be accomplished relatively quickly and easily.

7. To live by the values Jesus lived by, a Christian has to _____ himself, take up his _____, and _____ Jesus.

8. True ___ or False ___: We Christians are not alone as we reform our values. God has given us His Word to tell us what needs changing and how it is to be changed. He has also given us the indwelling of His Holy Spirit to empower the change, and He has given us other Christians to encourage us.

Bibliography

Adams, Jay. *A Theology of Christian Counseling*. Grand Rapids: Zondervan, 1979.

---. *Godliness Through Discipline*. Grand Rapids: Baker Book House, 1972.

---. *Lectures on Counseling*. Grand Rapids: Baker Book House, 1977. .

---. *The Christian Counselor's Manual*. Phillipsburg: Presbyterian and Reformed Publishing Company, 1973.

Almy, Gary. *How Christian Is Christian Counseling?* Wheaton: Crossway Books, 2000. .

Bobgan, Martin, and Deidre Bobgan. *The Psychological Way/ The Spiritual Way*. Minneapolis: Bethany Fellowship Inc., 1978.

Coffman, Burton. *Proverbs. The Wisdom Literature 2*. Abilene: ACU Press, 1993.

Collins, Gary. *Christian Counseling*. Waco: Word Books, 1980.

Geisler, Norman, and Ron Brooks. *When Skeptics Ask*. Grand Rapids: Baker Books, 1990.

Grudem, Wayne, and Jerry Thacker. *Why Is My Choice of a Bible Translation So Important?* Louisville: The Council on Biblical Manhood and Womanhood, 2005.

Heathfield, Susan. "Success in Life and Work." June 29, 2008. Online: http://www.humanresources.about.com/od/success/qt/values_s7.htm

Nelson, Dick. "Values and Behavior Change: Pastoral Psychology and Christian Education." *Journal of Psychology and Theology* (1979).

Posner, Roy. "The Power of Personal Values." June 29, 2008. Online: http://gurusoftware.com/Guru Net/Personal/Topics/Values.htm.

Poythress, Vern, and Wayne Grudem. *The Gender-Neutral Bible Controversy.* Nashville: Broadman & Holman Publishers, 2004.

Roach, Tony. *You Are God's Love Bank.* Abilene: God's Love Bank Enterprises, Inc., 2003.

Sander, Phil. *Adrift: Postmodernism in the Church.* Nashville: Gospel Advocate Company, 2000.

Walton, Rus. *Biblical Solutions to Contemporary Problems.* Arlington Height: Christian Liberty Press, 1988.

Williams, Scott. "Clarifying and Applying Personal Values: Priorities and Integrity." June 29, 2008. Online: http://www.wright.edu/~scitt.williams/skills/values.htm.

Endnotes

1. Gary Collins, *Christian Counseling* (Waco: World Books, 1980), 429.

2. Charles Swindoll, *Leadership*, Vol. 16, no. 2

3. Rus Walton, *Biblical Solutions to Contemporary Problems,* (Arlington Height: Christian Liberty Press, 1988), 1.

4. Norman Geisler and Ron Brooks, *When Skeptics Ask* (Grand Rapids: Baker Books, 1990), 157–159.

5. Ibid., 159–161.

6. "Episcopal Priest Ann Holmes Redding Has Been Defrocked," *The Seattle Times,* April 1, 2009.

7. http://www.merriam-webster.com, Online Dictionary, 2009.

8. Albert Mohler, "Criminalizing Christianity: Sweden Hate Speech Law," http://www.albertmohler.com/commentary-readphp?date=2004-08-05.

9. Radio program, "The Lutheran Hour."

10. Gary Almy, *How Christian Is Christian Counseling?* (Wheaton: Crossway Books, 2000), 17.

11. Vern S. Poythress and Wayne A. Grudem, *The TNIV and The Genger – Neutral Bible Controversy* (Nashville: Broadman & Holman Publishers, 2004), 167.

12. Roy Posner, "The Power of Personal Values," June 29, 2008, http://gurusoftware.com/Guru_Net/Personal/Topics/Values.htm.

13. Scott Williams, "Clarifying and Applying Personal Values: Priorities and Integrity," June 29, 2008, http://www.wright.edu/~scott.williams/skills/values.htm.

14. *American Heritage Dictionary, Third Edition.*

15. Roy Posner, "The Power of Personal Values," June 29, 2008, http://gurusoftware.com/Guru_Net/Personal/Topics/Values.htm.

16. Tony Roach, *You Are God's Love Bank* (Abilene: God's Love Bank Enterprises, Inc., 2003), 60

17. Ibid., 60-61

18. Dick Nelson, "Values and Behavior Change: Pastoral Psychology and Christian Education," *Journal of Psychology and Theology,* 1979, 212–219.

19. Ibid., 212-219

20. Scott Williams, "Clarifying and Applying Personal Values: Priorities and Integrity," June 29, 2008, http://www.wright.edu/~scitt.williams/skills/values.htm.

21. Tony Roach, *You Are God's Love Bank,* (Abilene: God's Love Bank Enterprises, Inc., 2003), 72-73.

22. Tony Roach, *You Are God's Love Bank* (Abilene: God's Love Bank Enterprises, Inc., 1993), 74.

23. Ibid., 1993, 76.

24. Ibid., 1993, 78.

25. Ibid., 1993, 81.

26. Ibid., 1993, 84.

27. Ibid., 1993, 84.

28. Ibid., 1993, 86.

29. Ibid., 1993, 89.

30. Spiro Zodhiates, *The Complete Word Study New Testament* (Chattanooga: AMG Publishers, 1991), 959.

31. Tony Roach, *You Are God's Love Bank* (Abilene: God's Love Bank Enterprises, Inc., 1993), 91

32. *American Heritage Dictionary, Third Edition.*

33. Tony Roach, *You Are God's Love Bank* (Abilene: God's Love Bank Enterprises, Inc., 1993), 93

34. Roach, 1993, 96

35. *American Heritage Dictionary,* Third Edition

36. Tony Roach, *You Are God's Love Bank* (Abilene: God's Love Bank Enterprises, Inc., 1993), 98

37. Saint Augustine of Hippo (AD 354–430).

38. Spiros Zodhiates , *The Complete Word Study New Testament* (Chattabiiga: AMB Publishers, 1992), 939.

39. Burton Coffman, *Proverbs. The Wisdom Literature 2* (Abilene: ACU Press, 1993), 51

40. Jay Adams, *Godliness Through Discipline* (Grand Rapids: Baker Book House, 1972), 15–16.

41. Ibid., 4–5.

LaVergne, TN USA
25 February 2010
174282LV00001B/39/P